Against Democracy

Against Democracy

Literary Experience in the Era of Emancipations

Simon During

FORDHAM UNIVERSITY PRESS

NEW YORK 2012

Fordham University Press also publishes its books in a variety of electronic formats. Some content that appears in print may not be available in electronic books.

Library of Congress Cataloging-in-Publication Data

During, Simon, 1950–

Against democracy : literary experience in the era of emancipations / Simon During.
p. cm.
Includes bibliographical references and index.
ISBN 978-0-8232-4254-2 (hardback) —
ISBN 978-0-8232-4255-9 (paper)
1. Literature—History and criticism—Theory, etc.
2. Democracy in literature. 3. Conservatism in literature.
4. Politics and literature. I. Title.
PN441.D797 2012
809'.933582—DC23

2011046356

Printed in the United States of America

14 13 12 5 4 3 2 1

First edition

CONTENTS

PREFACE

This book asks: How democratic *is* literature? And it answers: Barely at all, not politically. At least until recently. Which is where its strongest—or at any rate boldest—claims kick in. Literary history, I contend, is to be treasured today just because literature has historically been so suspicious of political democracy. Admittedly, for the past couple of centuries or so, literature has also assiduously engaged democratic life, systematically so in the case of the modern novel. But with some important exceptions it has represented that life skeptically, ambiguously, uneasily, darkly. Where it has strengthened democracy, it has done so mainly by resisting or questioning it.

Literature is to be treasured for its counterdemocratic force because it has now become so difficult—I personally find it impossible—to affirm political democracy's promise. History eroded that promise during the era of emancipations that started in 1776 and 1789, and especially in the phase of modernization, which started around 1830 in western Europe, when democracy was simultaneously and slowly integrated into an international system of state capitalism and then gradually extended into everyday life and into experience itself. Toward the end of that process, political democracy became a core component in a global system's apparatus of self-reproduction and self-management. So any progressivist demand for more and more democracy as organized through the state became, in effect if not intent, a demand for more and more of what we already have. And that is a problem. To take just one instance, with democracy's and capitalism's moment of ultimate world triumph around 1989, it became impossible to overlook the fact that their alliance had failed and would all but certainly continue to fail to generate sufficient security, justice, community solidarity, and material resources to provide a dependably good life for vast numbers of people around the world. However difficult this may be to concede, there's no evidence to suggest that more or "better" political or cultural democracy would change the situation.

Otherwise put, it would appear that political democracy has become compulsory now that viable social and political alternatives to the alliance between democracy and capitalism have apparently vanished, and there is indeed a sense in which history has ended—but not happily. This means that those who wish fully to inherit our most powerful social, literary, and spiritual heritages can no longer be, in any joyful way, democrats. Understood "postdemocratically," then (that is, understood from a position that today finds almost no support), literature's abiding conservatism is now a reservoir, if not exactly of hope or radical will, then at least of experiences and values at odds with (or even incommensurate with) current social conditions. This perception leads toward a revisioning of the history of conservatism itself, a task I begin below. But more important, at least for me here, it means that literature may become an instrument to distance or remove us, if only virtually, from the flawed regime that now, in its various modes and structures, covers the globe. This book argues that literature becomes a particularly powerful political instrument when, in the form of the novel, it most carefully and critically engages with democracy, in part, as I shall argue, because it has also found or imagined other minor democracies—conversational democracies—that can supplement or reprimand the values of political democracies in place.

This argument—which roams over political theory, literary history, and criticism; intellectual history and cultural studies; and which serves a complex, if pessimistic, left-conservative (or, if you prefer, nonprogressive left) political judgment—has been developed and thickened in classrooms and lecture halls in North America and Australia over the past three or four years. Admittedly, aspects of this line of thought, and in particular its reading of the current geopolitical situation, are set out in the final chapter of my last book, *Exit Capitalism*. But *Exit Capitalism*'s political and literary-historical implications are reformulated here in ways that largely respond to discussions I have had since writing it.

Against Democracy is based most of all on the three lectures on "Democracy and Literature" delivered as the Ward-Phillips Lecture Series at the University of Notre Dame, South Bend, Indiana, in 2009, which now constitute the book's last three chapters—on Benjamin Disraeli, Alexis de

Tocqueville, George Eliot, E. M. Forster, and Saul Bellow. I thank David Thomas and John Sitter for their encouragement and generosity as hosts. The current form of the chapter on reformism and revolution was talked over at the New School in New York in 2008, an invitation I owe to Dom Pettman and Ken Wark, and then again for a seminar on culture and secularism at Columbia University's Heywood Center for the Humanities, where Gauri Viswanathan was my attentive and thoughtful host. The chapter on Forster was given at the Yale English Department and at EMSAH at the University of Queensland, and it was workshopped at the Cornell School of Criticism and Theory (SCT) in June 2009, invitations I owe respectively to Michael Warner, Gillian Whitlock, and Amanda Anderson. Chapter 4, on the history of modern literary criticism, was also presented at the SCT at that time. My thoughts about conservatism were developed in a seminar on "Conservatism, Religion, History," at the SCT once more, and then, further, in a graduate class at Johns Hopkins, and, thanks to Julian Murphet's enthusiasm, refined again at the University of New South Wales, where in August 2010 I gave a talk that forms the basis of the second chapter here. My sense of Bellow owes much to an informative conversation I had on the topic with Martin Jay early in 2010—which is not to imply that he would agree with my argument here. In November of that year, I organized a stimulating seminar on culture and democracy at CHED at the University of Queensland (my current academic home), which was attended by Mark Andrejevic, Justin Clemens, Catherine Driscoll, Gay Hawkins, Peter Holbrook, Ian Hunter, Paul Patton, and David Pritchard, where these ideas on democracy underwent further shocks and changes. My sincere thanks to those who attended that event. Two incisive manuscript readers' reports, which, as I now know, were written by Bruce Robbins and Amanda Anderson, were decisive in leading me further to develop my analysis and its presentation.

This book is dedicated to my wife, Lisa O'Connell, and to my daughter, Nell During, who, generously, have paid the price of the time and energy it has absorbed, as well as, perhaps, the state of mind in which it was written.

ONE

Democracy Today

Literature and democracy? It's a topic that only a few years ago would have seemed remote from what was most urgent in the academic humanities. But the situation has changed. Democracy in particular solicits our attention. The perennial stream of books and articles across various disciplines addressing democracy's successes and failures has become a flood.[1] Republicans, associationalists, classical liberals, social democrats, and conservatives have all registered their sense that democracy needs to be reconstituted (Balibar 2010, Gauchet 2007, Hirst 1994, Runciman 2005, Skinner 1998). Influential radical European philosophers have also been actively engaged in retheorizing the concept, for the most part by defining it as a name for a regime in which all identities and substances whatsoever are open to political inspection and discussion (Badiou 2006, Rancière 2006, Derrida 2006). In the wake of this outpouring of commentary, it has become clear that democracy engages us so urgently today because it is at a transformative (and perhaps culminating) moment in its history.

We can think of this moment under two aspects.[2] From the one side, over the last few decades, political democracy has become almost wholly reconciled to capitalism. The possibility of a democratic system that might nationalize large swathes of the economy for good has disappeared. No viable political agenda proposes radically to redistribute wealth. Spirited, anticapitalist, organized activism has vanished: interventions like John. L. Lewis's defiance of Franklin D. Roosevelt (when, under sustained attack from the media, the politicians, and the big trade unions, he organized a coal strike in the middle of World War II) are now all but inconceivable in any developed or developing country (for Lewis, see James 1993, 269). Which is to say that, despite important national and regional differences in how governments and markets interact with one another, democratic processes are increasingly an instrument of "market states" the world over.[3]

As such, contemporary democratic state capitalism (as we can peremptorily call the system as a whole) is marked by the unprecedented degree to which its components have become technologically and ideologically integrated.[4] These components include the market, including the operations of finance capital; the forces of material, intellectual, and cultural production, especially the media, the Internet, and educational institutions; the machinery of welfare and social security; juridical and penal systems; and, indeed, religion, perhaps not least in the modernizing force of global Pentecostalism.[5]

The historical forces that are propelling the integration of these diverse domains are too various and multileveled to be currently fully available to analysis, although the arguments behind Joseph Schumpeter's *Capitalism, Socialism, and Democracy* (1942) remain suggestive. Schumpeter predicted that, in the postwar era, liberal capitalism would in effect merge with democratic socialism and that the "institutional framework" of the high-bourgeois liberalism inherited from the nineteenth century would be shed (Schumpeter 1950, 150ff.). In making his case, he pointed out that innovation and social reform were both becoming "automatic" (that is, bureaucratic and administrative rather than political and charismatic) and that finance capital was coming under the control of corporations and associations like pension funds rather than of individuals. From within capitalism, ownership and control of the means of production was effectively being democratized and integrated into the state. Today it is important to recognize that that integration is also required to manage what the German ecologist and sociologist

Ulrich Beck, in his prescient book *Risk Society: Towards a New Modernity* (1986), called "reflexive modernization," by which he meant the continually shifting demand imposed upon modernizing forces to manage the social and environmental damage and risk that they cause to nature and themselves (Beck 1992, 12–15). Democratic state capitalism has become so tightly integrated partly to protect itself from the world and the world from itself.

At the same time, the political system appears incoherent. Official purposes have become radically disjunct from actual effects. In particular, as policy options for political parties have narrowed (and, in the United States though not elsewhere, as party discipline was weakened by administrative reforms in the 1970s), they have become largely detached from the historicophilosophical beliefs that originally (at least supposedly) inspired them.[6] Their traditional constituencies can be decreasingly taken for granted. Most often, parties, which nonetheless find consensus as difficult to achieve as ever, scheme to win power from one another by attempting to manipulate a mediascape only intermittently attentive to formal politics—and rarely to policy itself. To use the lexicon of the eighteenth century, interests are (once again) swamping principles. Yet the issues at stake in the political process still involve questions of life and death for large numbers of people (as in debates over immigration or how health care should be funded and organized). In this wash of forces and interests, the political processes and institutions in which parties enact their differences are perceived as insensitive to actual social wants. They appear to many to have been effectively dedemocratized. This situation has been named "postdemocracy" or "democracy against itself" (Dunn 2005, 186–187; Rancière 1999, 95–121; Gauchet 2007, 14).

On the other side, democracy—or, better, democratization—has become compulsory. Democracy is now, as John Dunn notes, the only "legitimate basis for political authority," backed by those historians and sociologists who affirm an essential link between democratization, historical emancipation, and modernization (Dunn 2005, 15; for the democracy-equals-modernization argument, see Inglehart and Welzel 2005, Sen 2000, Tilly 2004, and Keane 2009). Alternatives to democracy—theocracy, say, from the radical right, or autonomism from the radical left—are granted neither legitimacy nor presence: they are practically impossible.[7] So most of the actually existing critics of democracy are democrats who call for "radical democracy" or "redemocratization"[8] (Surin 2009, 15). Or for more democracy: Bruno Latour, for instance, even calls for a new modality of democracy that extends to "things"—by which he means a political system that sufficiently acknowledges the social agency of the inorganic and technological (Latour 1993, 12). Democracy here exceeds the human.

One reason that democracy has become our primary political standard is that it now functions to legitimize the incoherent system as much as to govern it (see Canfora 2006, 227, for a version of this argument). Democratic state capitalism tightly binds parts that adhere to universal norms of justice to those parts that don't. And democracy is as much a promise and an imagined idea with its own traditions and genealogies as it is a governmental arrangement, and it is as an idea that it fulfills the system's need for legitimization. It has become a talisman: its own self-generating, constituting force. Nonetheless, it is the system's practical or promised ability to extend (or even just to maintain) prosperity and security, which belongs as much to the market as to the state, that effectively allows democratic state capitalism to bury the possibility of thoroughgoing structural transformation.

Because no alternative system can be realistically worked toward, let alone achieved through revolution, we can think of the system as "endgame capitalism," too (During 2010, 131–160). As far as it is possible to see, democratic state capitalism is now, bar paranoia, seriously threatened only by sovereign nature. It stands presented as global society's final horizon. But this does not mark the end of history as progressivism imagined it. It cannot be claimed that either emancipation or human potential has now been maximally achieved. It cannot be persuasively supposed that the democratic idea joined to capitalism will ever in fact order a society as just and good as we can imagine a society to be.

So it is difficult to accept Theodor Adorno's claim (made in 1956) that "the horror is that for the first time we live in a world in which we can no longer imagine a better one" (Adorno and Horkheimer 2010, 61). The problem is not imagining a better society; the problem is realizing it. After all, endgame capitalism cannot be reconciled to the bourgeois secular theodicy tradition that began with Leibniz in the seventeenth century, for which history delivers us the best possible social system.[9] It is not, as I say, a Hegelian condition of *posthistoire*, in which rational universal norms have been implemented, or even a Kojèvean one, for which the divisive reign of desire has been supplanted by the peaceful reign of mere satisfactions and interests. Rather, our polity seems to be under the sway of that "neutralization" which Carl Schmitt believed to characterize social democracy, a condition in which struggles between rival constitutional and economic systems—struggles for which lives are willingly staked—has given way to policy debates predominantly carried out by experts, as well as to politics delivered over to those who in the 1950s came to be called the "mass persuaders" (Schmitt 1996).

In effect, democratic state capitalism ends history prematurely. Or rather: it propels us toward living without strong historical hope. For all that, however, I do think that it is useful, in a somewhat Hegelian spirit, to regard endgame capitalism as (for itself) fusing the laws of nature with the order of history, since it is as if, as Michel Foucault has argued of nineteenth-century liberalism, contemporary society—legitimized by a democratic idea seconded to the commitment to capital growth—understands itself as an expression not so much of God's mandate for the world but rather as of the way things *are*, whether rationally or ontologically or merely historically (Foucault 2008, 15–16). It belongs to the "natural order of things," as Adam Smith said of the historical development of commerce (Smith 1993, 230). Or as John Dewey put it in a moment of metaphysically ambitious democratic enthusiasm, "Nature itself, as that is uncovered and understood by our best contemporaneous knowledge, sustains and supports our democratic hopes and aspirations" (cited in Westbrook 1991, 320). Here Dewey invokes nature (against reason) as democratic society's absolute ontological ground, and it is the echo of that kind of understanding, however faint, that today seals history's premature end.

At the same time as democracy has come to monopolize political normativity, it has expanded into cultural, domestic, and sexual life. Since the end of World War II, and especially since 1968, propelled by both market and political forces, the various social zones in which we can engage in free and personal practices of self and that shape the mood and protocols of everyday life have been further subjected to democratization. There has been a melting of inherited structures and habits, a broader distribution of self-confidence, and a firmer resistance to judgments that hierarchize and discriminate. Pretty much any social identity whatsoever can be recognized and granted rights. In sum, we are involved in what Karl Mannheim long ago named "fundamental democracy," democracy that is maximizing its reach into culture and civil society (Mannheim 1940, 53ff.). Perhaps most prominent among democratic fundamentalism's various trajectories has been the democratization of manners and culture—the overcoming of deference and rank markers in ordinary social exchange (which I will call "conversational democracy") and the belief that all cultural forms have equal value and should invite equal access (which I will call "cultural democracy").[10]

Democratization also imprints itself on experience itself, where we think of experience both as personal existence's lived feel and meaning and as the constitutive, nondivisible particle of a philosophical anthropology. That philosophical anthropology, which was worked out by Thomas Hobbes and John Locke in the seventeenth century, imagines consciousness as the combination of various kinds of experiences (as "sensations," "impressions," "ideas"), some present, some remembered, some imagined, some private, some social or conversational. Experience becomes the center of democracy theory when further analyzed by thinkers such as Ralph Waldo Emerson, William James, and John Dewey, in a tradition for which it becomes nothing less than nature's vehicle of self-revelation (see Dewey 2008, 12–13). The category is so attractive to democrats because experiences seem to precede tradition, learning, hierarchies, and morality.[11] In particular, while knowledge hierarchizes, experiences do not, and while morality divides and limits (some people will always fail its tests), experiences do not. It is in these terms, for instance, that the eighteenth-century English novelist Henry Fielding, writing for an expanding reading public and for commercial booksellers, famous for a life "spent in promiscuous intercourse with persons of *all* ranks," as a friend remarked, in *Tom Jones* nominates "Experience" as one of the novel form's indispensable muses (Battestin 1989, 145). Furthermore, experiences, which just are and which happen (it appears) serially, more or less contingently, are *like* democratic citizens who enter into their privileges simply by being born, one after another, in a particular place at a particular time, and who need share little. From within this logic democracy goes further, and it tends to offer experience itself as a basic criterion of value, as if societies are good just to the degree that they deliver rich and full experiences rather than to the degree that, say, they encourage virtuous living or offer social order or unity or purpose. This is possible because experiences can be understood as valuable whether or not they serve any universal purposes or instantiate any universal structures, or whether or not they have particular relations to other experiences or even to the world. Taken to its limits, as William James does at the beginning of the twentieth century, a philosophy of "pure experience" supports (or as James put it, "harmonizes best with") the radical democratic pluralism that has become the most solidly sanctioned form of political organization, at least for academic intellectuals (James 2000, 336). Closer to our own time, Richard Rorty has made a similar case, arguing that a democracy self-directed toward the future as contingency, democracy with no project in view and appealing to no established and static principle or authorities, is the political expression of a philosophy that has abandoned all metaphysics. It is the political correlate of a philosophy whose only touchstone is accumulated experience (see Rorty 1998, 1–39). American democracy (at any rate in its idealized form) becomes the instantiation of this minimalist philosophic rationality.

What is the relation between compulsory and fundamental democracy? It is clearly mediated by the market and the state, especially the massification of the education and media spheres and the implementation of equal-opportunity legislation. The relatively wide sharing of affluence (by historical standards) that enables sustained economic growth, backed by the industrial production of consumer goods, also produces a certain cultural flattening, through mechanisms that need no spelling out.[12] At the same time, however, we can easily imagine a historical condition in which democracy and capitalism are regarded as the only legitimate or natural arrangements of society that nonetheless remains oligarchic and that in which, further, the rich classes are marked off from the rest of society by their self-ascribed higher culture, their more civilized manners, their more refined sensibilities, and their capacities for subtler, deeper experiences. Close to the beginnings of political theory as a philosophic mode, Aristotle believed such a combination of oligarchy and democracy to be definitive of life in the city (that is, the polity), and indeed, incoherently, we today still live in such a regime. If we did not, then a sociological analysis such as Pierre Bourdieu's in *Distinction* (1979), which argues that only elites have the capacity to appreciate objects aesthetically, would not acquire its plausibility. So the relation between compulsory and fundamental democracy would appear to be neither quite necessary nor quite contingent. We might say that it is subject to complex and mysterious connections and rhythms that aesthetic models best catch. In particular, whatever else it is, the relation between various democratic drives is mimetic. The idea of equality especially is emulated, tried out, as if by contagion, across different social and cultural zones, where it fits better sometimes than others. Or, if you prefer, democracy and equality vibrate from one zone to another in a fitful Pythagorean music of secular spheres.

Even democracy that is becoming fundamental is bounded. It needs to limit itself in order to maintain itself. Thus—to offer two concrete examples—at the level of the state itself, it's not undemocratic to withdraw judicial appointments from democratic processes or for electoral boundaries to be decided nondemocratically, to avoid gerrymandering. But, more important, democratizing processes fall short in major social sectors. In civil society, democracy halts in the family: relations between parents and children can't be wholly governed by principles of liberty and equality and can't simply be ordered by appeal to the equality of experiences qua experiences, either. The legal system, too, is rarely ordered by democratic principles. Democracy also, and increasingly, halts in workplaces, especially in bureaucracies and large corporations (and in universities as well), as Schmitt contended against Max Weber and Hans Kelsen in the 1920s and as Harry Braverman demonstrated beyond reasonable doubt in the 1970s (Schmitt 1985, 24–25; Braverman 1974). At the same time, the unimpeded market tirelessly de-creates and re-creates inequality. To state this argument in general terms: democracy is often *contained* by institutional, economic, and mundane life. Indeed, it can be argued, as does Pierre Rosanvallon, that "counterdemocracy"—the persistent, more or less institutional *distrust* of democracy—forms, and always has formed, a constitutive element of modern democracy itself (Rosanvallon 2008b). It could also be more radically argued that democracy's monopolization of political legitimacy provides cover for actual dedemocratization.

A form of counterdemocracy extends into the experiential itself. As Ellen Meiksins Wood has noted, "huge expanses of our human life—in fact most of our daily experience" happens "outside the ambit of democracy, even in principle, let alone in practice" (Wood 1991, 176). While experience may be shaped by and shape democracy, while experience may be ontologically analogous to democratic citizenship, while experience may now function both as a telos and as a norm, and while democracy may become experience and affect's vehicle (about a century ago, the German phenomenologist Max Scheler invented a name for this—moody democracy, or *Stimmungsdemokratie*), while all this is the case, nonetheless experience's modes—of love and hate, hope and fear, violence and compassion, need and content, grief and joy, trust and betrayal, ambition and desire, ascesis and abandon, will and submission—are also other to democracy (for Scheler, see Mannheim 1956, 175). Whether feelings and consciousness bind or separate us, they neither free us nor make us equal in any politically or socially applicable way *as* feeling and consciousness. I suspect that it is because they intuit this experiential resistance to democracy that some contemporary theorists—Anthony Giddens, for instance—have called for a "life politics" to institute a "democracy of the emotions in everyday life," that is, to install democratic decision-making processes that explicitly include emotions as well as opinions and reason (Giddens 1994, 16). However that may be, there remains a residual tension between democratic subjectivity and the democratic idea, or, to state this more accurately, between everyday life under democracy and the democratic "ethos," where, along the lines spelled out by Foucault, we think of that ethos as the affective and/or discursive structure that underpins and maintains democratic societies as democratic (for "ethos," see Foucault 1994, 571–578; also, Geuss 2005, 153–161).

It's remarkable that the combination of (1) the disappearance of strong rivals to democratic capitalism as a political good, (2) the de- or nondemocratization of many actual governmental and business institutions, and (3) the simultaneous expansion of and check to democratic norms into the life-world have occurred simultaneously across much of the developed world. Where—as notably in China—liberal political democracy is rejected (though not ideals of popular sovereignty and egalitarianism), legitimacy is still ascribed by referring to how much democratic potential across a range of life zones the system shelters (see Wang 2003). Where democratic state capitalism as such is not in place at all—in North Korea, for example—the global community withholds legitimacy and, often, material support, unless such states (for example, Saudi Arabia) happen to be U.S. clients. The so-called Arab Spring, which occurred as this manuscript was finished, is, I think, to be understood as an event in which revolutions from below are drawing some such states into the system of democratic state capitalism on the high, "free," Western model, further extending that model's reach.

By my reckoning, only a careful historical narrative sensitive to national and regional differences as well as to the play between structure and contingency, in which the relatively recent dates 1945, 1968, 1989, 2001, and 2008 would figure prominently, can account for this shapeless conjuncture. It cannot be adequately explained theoretically or structurally, since what is required to understand it is an immersion in the situations out of which fundamental democracy in particular has been and is being constructed, and an immersion from a particular and accounted-for position at that. (See Gauchet 2007, 12–13, for a similar point.)

In this book, I want to clarify how democratization, understood in the terms that I have been outlining, works historically in relation to high culture and, in particular, in relation to literary high culture, leaving aside, for the moment, the question of what we might actually mean by "literary high culture." And in broaching this topic, we soon make a surprising finding. Although insights like William Blake's that all men "are alike in the Poetic Genius" do help organize moments both in modern democracy and in modern literature, those moments play a relatively minor role. As the French literary critic Alfred Thibaudet recognized early in the twentieth century, literature has positioned itself *against* more than *with* democratization (Thibaudet 1913, 5). Up until 1945, in Europe at least, few canonical writers and literary critics were democrats, and many were democracy's avowed and, in this context, conservative enemies. But, as I will suggest, this literary conservatism seems to have encouraged democratization as much as it impeded it.

We can crudely outline the larger logics of this connection between literature and democracy like this: Serious literature was, and is, mainly written and read by the educated and the relatively rich and powerful, and therefore it has been allied, albeit loosely, to dominant social fractions who have tended to resist the processes of egalitarianism in particular. So it often draws its energies both from those spheres of society and everyday life where democracy does not govern as well as from memories of a nondemocratic past. At the same time, under democratization, literature too became more and more focused on experiences as such. This creates another tension. After all, literature aims to bring us sublimity or hard-won truths and insights, or a picture of an ideal order, or a brush with transcendence, or signal passions and sympathies—serious literature aims to be *exceptional*—and, for that reason, it fears and seeks to evade supersession by democratic ordinariness. Modern literature may indeed, as Jacques Rancière argues, inaugurate a "democracy of the letter"—that is, an indifference to old hierarchies of genre, style, and topic—but that kind of literary democracy contains no particular relation to political or social democracy. Indeed, as Rancière himself recognizes, in writers like Flaubert literary democracy understood this way may be positioned *against* political democracy (Rancière 2009b, 504). In the end, even modern, dehierarchized literature still strains toward aesthetic or experiential exceptionality. More than that, there remains a sense in which no regime can be imagined as less hospitable to, less able to *read*, literature than one that is fundamentally democratic, a situation that writers like Maurice Blanchot, for example (as we will see), can choose to embrace. We can think of it like this: that the arts could only flourish in conditions of substantive freedom was a commonplace of classical thought (Tacitus, Longinus), and, from that point of view, and given that our current social system cannot provide the leisure, carefreeness, and freedom enjoyed by, for instance, the citizens (*not* the inhabitants) of Athens or republican Rome, how can we today expect to recognize and admire art and literature's full force? At any rate, even as it too joins the democratizing stream, the flow from artistic and literary representations to the idioms of democratic everyday life and back is often guarded and frictional, if not always so.

In sum, twentieth-century literary high culture, in particular, was largely shaped in the rhythms and forms through which it adapted to and resisted its translation into and out of mundane experience as ordered in (sometimes merely emergent) democratic state capitalism. Yet images of democratic life are rarely thicker than they are in good literary writing; the possibilities for new and different pathways for democratic contagion, for new (dangerous or not) democratic relations, can rarely be presented more concretely than in imaginative literature. So the democratic idea itself often becomes vivid, imagined into the realm of experience, through the work of its victims, critics, and enemies (especially its "intimate enemies," to use Ashis Nandy's term) as well as of its friends. That's one important way in which democracy is literary conservatism's child too.

It is on the basis of this understanding of democracy, and also because I sense that we don't have enough democracy where we need it and too much where we don't, that I want to use terms such as "compulsory democracy," "democratic fundamentalism," and "endgame capitalism" as gestures to a future that extends beyond democracy, even if that future can only be anticipated from a position almost without content, that is to say, by emptied social hope. It's from that contentless place that I want to explore certain moments in democracy's literary history. This claim also immediately articulates a further relation to conservatism (as I will spell out in more detail in Chapter 3), since it is an important effect of democracy's monopolization of politics and the life-world that would-be dissidents so quickly find themselves in conservatism, conceived of as an attachment to what is being lost under modernizing processes. What's left, otherwise, except more democracy? So it is important to recognize that, in the epoch of compulsory democracy, conservatism cannot be reduced to the programs of the political right.[13]

As will already be apparent, *Against Democracy* combines intellectual history, political theory, and literary criticism as brought together under a particular understanding and judgment of contemporary society. Perhaps a little oddly, it becomes more directly concerned with literature as it proceeds. That's just because I have felt that the difficult question of how to position oneself critically in regard to democracy today requires not just extended working out but careful historical and institutional placement. This is the task of my next three chapters, each of which focuses on a specific relation between democracy and the literary humanities in particular. The following three chapters turn more directly to creative writers and texts.

In Chapter 2, I begin by arguing the case for the cogency of a particular politicoethical position—a bicameral or split one that simultaneously refuses compulsory democracy and at the same time works to reform it—and I use my affirmation of this position as a springboard to describe chapters of the intellectual/literary history that have made such a position all but invisible among academic theorists and critics. I concentrate first on Michel Foucault's lectures on the 1940s origins of neoliberalism and, next, on twentieth-century philosophical antihumanism, especially in Maurice Blanchot's work, as Blanchot's revolutionary ultra-right politics of the interwar period mutated into an influential model of the literary itself. My third chapter turns away from the reform/revolution opposition to the concept of critique, and in doing so makes the case that, in the wake of critique's failure, conservatism hails us. It makes this case by examining two early twentieth-century theories of conservatism, Karl Mannheim's *Conservatism: A Contribution to the Sociology of Knowledge* and Carl Schmitt's *Political Romanticism*, each of which focuses on literature and culture. Chapter 4 stays with a certain conservatism, since it offers a revisionary description of modern literary criticism, which, I contend, was aimed largely toward discriminating between experiences in a situation where, so the critics thought, experience itself was being debased by democratic modernization. At the beginning, literary criticism attempted to install a counterdemocratic relation to culture into the democratic state itself. This chapter is important to the book's overall argument, since not only do I remain in qualified sympathy with that original mode of modern literary criticism but, in the following chapters, also see it as indirectly shaping later literature itself.

It is at this point that I turn to literature more properly. Chapter 5 examines the period when literature (in Alexis de Tocqueville, Benjamin Disraeli, and George Eliot) first encountered the general realization among European writers and intellectuals that democracy was inevitable. The sixth chapter examines a particular moment in democracy's interaction with literature—the moment when liberalism and so-called mystical democracy each intersected with social democracy in E. M. Forster's *Howards End* (1909). I argue that *Howards End* is not to be thought of as a liberal novel but as one that charts a distance between the emerging social democratic polity and a democratic ethos understood in something like Walt Whitman's terms. The last chapter turns to Saul Bellow's work—*Herzog* (1964), in particular—as a moment that illuminates a penultimate stage of literary culture's democratization and that also constitutes a new (delirious) stage in conservatism's accommodation to, and flight from, democratic experience and the democratic ethos.

TWO

Reform or Refusal? Living in Democratic Capitalism

Democracy's authority, its charisma of legitimacy, is so overwhelmingly strong that it is difficult to see how we might stand outside it. Yet it is not as if radical and crippling criticism of contemporary democratic society is rare in practice. And we can easily adduce three kinds of commonly remarked systemic failure: (1) distributional, (2) administrative, and (3) experiential.

Distributional failure concerns global democratic capitalism's long-term and continuing incapacity to prevent ongoing massive inequities in terms of income and access to resources and goods, for example, health care and education. (The most recent evidence for this continuing inequity and its wider social impact is to be found in Wilkinson and Pickett 2009.) And of course the immense difficulty of imagining how the whole of the planet's population might ever achieve the same standard of living of, say, the richest billion people today only sharpens this judgment.

Administrative failure concerns democratic government's increasing surveillance, quantification, and restrictive control of all its subjects, including its measures of exclusion. These include the building of walls and the deployment of militarized violence to prevent cross-border travel by workers, stateless persons, and refugees; the positive correlation between rates of incarceration and economic development; the extension of security agencies' power and extent; and the use of public and private computer networks to store information for purposes of manipulation and control, whether in commercial or state interests.

Experiential failure concerns democratic capitalism's inability to secure the social conditions (or habitus) in which individuals and collectives, even those safely inside the system, may live maximally good lives. Those conditions should provide, inter alia, a fit degree of confidence in the future; sufficient trust in the system's fairness and transparency, however fairness and transparency are parsed; and enough time, liberty, and resources for people to control their own lives and to pursue their chosen responsibilities and enjoyments. More arguably, democracy should also offer people the capacity to understand the (secular and nonsecular) settings and determinations of their lives as justified and coherent, if not purposive. As for the substance of the good life, we can accept the reigning secular definition of it as a life in which people may consistently and reliably enjoy fulfilling, subtle, and reflective experiences, where "experience" is understood as a situated state of consciousness in which thought, feeling, perception, memory, expectation, sociability, and creativity are variously fused and combined. Under this head, the claim is that while democracy leads us to figure the good life experientially and not, for instance, in terms of the virtues that it sustains or its adherence to traditions or to dignity or its closeness to God, at the same time, it, together with the market, actually debases experiences, partly because, as just noted, it does not provide the conditions of fairness, clarity, and coherence that allow experiences to flourish, and partly because it habitually overrides the potential richness of particular experiences by processes and structures that are designed to maximize exchange, utility, productivity, and profit.

Even as succinctly stated as this, these failures confront us with the political question that has long haunted state democratic capitalism: Should we flatly refuse the system as a whole and work for its radical overthrow and transformation, or should we instead work to reform it?

It should already be apparent what the *rational* response to this question is. The various retreats of alternatives to democracy—communism, guild socialism, integral monarchism, corporatism, and state socialism—mean that, in our time, no rational evasion of reformism is possible. In particular, few of us today believe in the political anthropology that upheld socialism, namely the "elemental" strength of the "instructive rebelliousness and creative force of the modern masses," as C. L. R. James put it (James 1993, 226). And few of us (other than the contemporary autonomists) believe that the "general intellect" (the socially produced store of knowledge and creativity) can itself work as an engine of emancipation. Right reason would rather have us join those ceaseless efforts to manage democratic capitalism's crises and growth spurts in the interests of social justice and the incremental, ceaseless diminution of poverty, prejudice, and suffering.

But is the rational response sufficient? In my view, the answer to that is also "no." Even if one cannot await revolution, one cannot simply resign oneself to the endless task of remitting state capitalism's insufficiencies. Endgame capitalism's incapacity to realize justice, security, and coherent clarity; its indifference to immiseration and precariousness; its degradation of experience and of intellectual and creative possibilities; its dispersion and wastage of energy are all just too savage. Then, too, the processes of reform can too easily become further instruments of destruction, as democratic capitalism endlessly renews itself by appropriating, and sometimes configuring itself around, its critique and dissent (for this argument, see Boltanski and Chiapello 2006). As I have already suggested, the demand for more or better democracy in particular only strengthens the system, since that demand no longer contains any strong anticapitalist implications. At best, it requests either more general participation in—or more state oversight over, or more state supplementation of—finance and the market. In this triple bind—neither revolution nor wholehearted reform nor the status quo—the terms that were once to hand to mount a resistance have vanished, while the motives to do so have not. And so, although the charges against reformism are themselves (to some degree) based on reason, the grounds for making an antireformist refusal are finally fideistic, just because, to repeat, neither an exit from nor a substantive alternative to democratic capitalism is imaginable. Ultimately, refusal is a blind leap into nothing.

In this situation, the difficult search to find concepts from which to refuse democratic capitalism, a search that does indeed end in a kind of existential wager, may move away from experience as a criterion of value to return to a vocabulary—to *names*—that, predating modernity, have not been wholly appropriated either by modern instrumentality and relativism or by any discourse and apparatus of universal norms as adapted to the system. Of course, to turn from critique toward memory in the effort to find grounds for judging the contemporary social system is difficult since, in our society, the passage of time absorbs, distorts, and expunges memories of other ways of life and other modes of experiencing, leaving us mainly with nostalgia. But still—words and things can pass from one era to another even if experiences cannot.

For me, the first such name that comes into view is that ancient philosophical word "perfection": *democratic state capitalism is not perfect enough to be endorsed on any grounds at all.* In making this suggestion, I am drawing on the philosophic tradition by appealing not to high Platonism but to an Aristotelian understanding of perfection as human action's (intermittently) realizable objective. That is to say, I am joining, from within a different social situation and to a different purpose, Matthew Arnold's affirmation of the quest for perfection as culture's final end. For Arnold, the concept of perfection energized collective and individual action toward cleaner, more intense and illuminated ways of life. It inspired practices of living and self-government that delivered themselves up to becoming rather than being and that were simultaneously personal and inward (in the general sense that they excluded no area of experience or action by fiat) and, last, were socially tolerant and harmonious rather than prescriptive. In its time, Arnoldian perfection thus stood against both the machinery of state administration and hard Christian moralism (Arnold 1965, 93ff.).

But, despite attempts to resuscitate it by Stanley Cavell in particular, Arnold's affirmation of perfection now lies in tatters, and in general it's apparent that history has produced notions of perfection that it is incapable not just of realizing but, as I say, of fully remembering and understanding. It is also clear that the speculative search for old names that might rebuke and judge contemporary society eschews the central question that faces us: how to position ourselves ethicopolitically in relation to compulsory democracy and endgame capitalism.

So I am arguing that if we want to pass what I'll call the "seriousness test," which measures political principles and purposes by their likely *practical* capacity to improve society—if we take reform's victory over revolution in that spirit—we are also led to take seriously our personal responsibility to endorse and join the process of social improvement. It is hard to escape the conclusion that within endgame capitalism we have a *duty* (to use another apparently dated concept) to improve the system so as to counter its distributional, administrative, and experiential failures. As it happens, however, this idea lies at the heart of Jacques Derrida's concept of a "democracy to come," since for him democracy is the duty, the *injunction*, as he more usually phrased it, to act politically, that is, to will freedom and equality beyond any limits (Derrida 1992, 38ff.). Perhaps more usefully, we can also parse this duty in the spirit of the British idealist F. H. Bradley as the necessity for us to acknowledge that we as individuals belong to society as a whole and that, in affirming this social interdependency "I affirm myself," as he put it (Bradley 1962, 163). To affirm oneself rationally and ethically entails a duty—a responsibility—to work for the society that enables us not just to live as we do but to be who we are. From within this tradition, T. S. Eliot would define democracy as a society in which "the maximum of responsibility is combined with the maximum of individual liberty" (Eliot 1965, 71). Or, otherwise put, to affirm oneself is to work, if possible, toward constructing the society in which we can most freely and fully occupy that responsible, serious self and, by the same stroke, most successfully escape external limitations on our experiences, wants, and purposes. In accepting that duty or responsibility, even those of us who would negate state democratic capitalism will find ourselves actively participating not just in local communitarianisms of one kind or another but also in the slow, misfiring, dirty, and limited business of party or union politics, just because there are no other practical paths to the lifting of barriers and restrictions and the alleviation of suffering and injustice.

Yet this serious participation, as I am saying, is to coexist with a rejection of the system itself, a system that touches all aspects of our lives from the family and "culture" to the workplace and public sphere—indeed to an unmappable extent, that reaches down into our experiences of the world. In sum, we are actively to participate in strengthening and legitimating a society whose foundations we reject, in the knowledge that our work may even, against its overt intent to improve, lead to further inequities and experiential destruction. Indeed, we have to recognize that there's a sense in which by making this move we are refusing ourselves too, at least to the degree that we are ourselves constituted socially. It is impossible to refuse society as it is currently organized without also refusing the refuser.

We should immediately note that this bicameral position, in which we are bound to both reform and refusal (and, hence, to emptied social hope), belongs to the deep abstract structures of Western (but not just Western) thought and practice. Here I am not thinking of irony or the cultivation of ambiguity as ethicospiritual attitudes, since they belong too much to the world. Nor am I thinking of those forms of Marxian "alienation" that reconcile being engaged in the world with emotional and intellectual distance from, and denunciation of, its social structures. I am, perhaps, closer to those classical modes of transcendentalism, whether Platonic or Kantian, which posit an unbridgeable distance between the ideal and the real or between the universal and the particular. But I want also to dissociate myself from transcendentalism on the grounds that the bicameralism that I am pointing to is not metaphysical and makes no ontological claims. It is situated and historical, its claims being staked where politics meets ethics. So the double consciousness that I am invoking lies nearer those practices of gnostic *Entweltlichung* (to use Rudolf Bultmann's word, literally "de-worlding") that reject the social world on the grounds that that world is experienced as *dürftig* (scanty, inadequate), a Heideggerian term usually—inadequately—translated into English as "destitute."

Consider the historically most important such practice, the relation between the Christian and society as laid down in the primitive Church. For instance, in one famous piece of pastoral instruction, Paul wrote, in what Giorgio Agamben describes as his "most vigorous definition of messianic life," that now "even those having wives may be as not having wives, and those rejoicing as not rejoicing and those that buy as not possessing, and those using the world as not using it up. For passing away is the figure of the world. But I wish you to be without care" (1 Corinthians 7:29–32; Agamben 2005, 22). Here, a proximate end of history—the messianic eschaton that deprives social existence of purpose—sucks the weeping out of weeping and the rejoicing out of rejoicing, so as to allow the faithful to live socially in conventional terms but "without care." It's a proposition that extends beyond Christianity well into the twentieth century, and literary intellectuals have often appealed to it. Here, for instance, is Maurice Blanchot writing (against Sartre) in the late 1940s: "to write is to be engaged; but to write is also be disengaged; to be engaged in the mode of irresponsibility" (Blanchot

1995, 26). Blanchot's irresponsibility is a nonalienated refusal that ultimately draws upon the Pauline Christian's being without care.

But such engagements without engagement did not have to cope with the duty to participate actively in reform processes. This is true even where it seems not to be. So, in another absolutely canonical text, Paul wrote, "Put them [that is, the faithful] in mind to be subject to principalities and powers, to obey magistrates, to be ready to every good work" (Titus 3:1). Here, Paul's instruction to obey secular powers is supplemented by the instruction actively to engage in good works, as if, in expectation of the end, the evacuation of the world could accompany its strengthening. Yet, in being enacted, the goodness is not being sucked out of goodness as the rejoicing is of rejoicing and the weeping is of weeping in the text from Corinthians, since this time the works of goodness either signify or attract God's grace with its promise of salvation.

Indeed, historically, the Pauline evacuation of the world anchored a very different politics than ours, the overturning of which was more or less constitutive of political modernity. After Luther (but not so much after Calvin, given Calvinism's theocratic tendencies), politics was sloganized around the phrases "nonresistance" and "passive obedience," namely the injunction to the faithful to obey all legitimate sovereigns, whether or not their injunctions were just. In his pastoral letter, the early Christian activist Peter (probably not to be identified with the apostle Peter) went so far as to claim that passive suffering under bad governors was sanctified as a type of Christ's own suffering (1 Peter 2:21). But the political efficacy of the doctrine of passive obedience was severely punctured by England's 1688 Glorious Revolution, when James II was overthrown with Tory and majority Anglican assent.[1] The importance of the year 1688 lies not just in its demission of nonresistance and divine right, not just in its establishing a mixed constitution that would survive to provide a model even for republican states to come but in its providing the political conditions under which the orthodox Christian subject could become the modern subject, that is, when the vertical, transcendental division between social being and being-for-God, between subject and soul, could become the horizontal, immanent distinction between the public and private self. It goes without saying that once *that* distinction regulates society, then the reform-versus-revolution dilemma is most easily avoided by retreat from the public into the private world. And, of course, to retreat into private life in that manner is to risk flouting one's duty to work to reform society.

Nonetheless, and this is what is truly startling, a strange desubstantiated form of passive obedience and nonresistance have returned to us, since, as I have implied, today sovereignty is ultimately ascribed to thought's ultimate grounds—not God this time but instead a present social condition (democratic state capitalism) in which historical development has been fused with a universal and immanent (if incoherent) rationality also inscribed in nature. This only intensifies the sense that we need to obey the system's explicit and implicit injunctions, not least the injunction to reform it, as if they have the force of what was once divine—that is to say, natural—law.

It is fairly clear why this position of simultaneously embracing refusal and reform has found so little traction. After all, its standards of judgment are high and remote, and its ethical and political consequences are difficult—perhaps impossible—to live out. Partly because in this particular form, and directed to these particular ends, it belongs to no established tradition or institution, it's all but contentless. One way to attempt to live out a reform-plus-refusal position might be to participate in high culture—especially literary high culture—as an effort to absorb the imaginative energies that are stored in high culture but that are also sufficiently foreign to democratic state capitalism to function as surrogates for harder-edged refusal, a participation that need not interrupt reformist, progressivist engagement. That, indeed, is a kind of literary subjectivity akin to what the earliest founders of modern academic literary criticism were reaching for, as we will see in Chapter 4. But given that possibility, a perplexing question remains. Why is it that the academic humanities in particular have for so long been so unaccommodating to reformism itself (the much easier side of this bicameral position to embrace) even though, outside the academy, reformism has won the battle against revolution? The moment when mainstream liberal progressivism did inspire important literary criticism, for instance—Lionel Trilling's and Richard Poirier's moment, let us say—was remarkably short-lived. As we shall see in the next chapter, one answer to the problem of truncated and sparse liberal reformism in literary studies is that the concept and practice of "critique" came to displace both reform and revolution for an influential group of Marxian intellectuals during the 1930s and 1940s, when reformism seemed inadequate at the very same time that revolution's impossibility became clearly apparent. Furthermore, since 1968, the classical reformist project was itself dissolved or marginalized as it was overtaken by emancipation movements on behalf of specific disenfranchised or oppressed groups, most notably women, people of color, and victims of colonialism, and in which the humanities did indeed play an important role. During the 1960s, a reinvigorated radicalism, along with identity politics, sidelined the urgency of reformism in the social democratic mode and sometimes reversed its political valency. As a result, reformism became parsed as conservative. Last, as the recent work of both Marcel Gauchet and Samuel Moyn has shown, in the aftermath of the 1960s the discourse of "human rights" suffused public and international policy discourse enough to sideline the urgency of social reform quite broadly (Gauchet 1989, Moyn 2010).

But such analyses do not adequately account for the fate of the reformist problematic in the post-1968 theory scene. Let me point to two other, closely connected intellectual formations that displaced reformism's appeal. This first was the attempt to develop radical methods and vocabularies outside of humanism and the socialist left—analyses whose key terms are *not* "capitalism" and "democracy." Michel Foucault's corpus stands as the most substantial and influential of these.[2] The second was the continuing seductive and displaceable appeal of revolution—not reformism—long after its practical political valency had evaporated, and here I'll focus on Maurice Blanchot's (also antihumanist) work, just because it came to be so deeply embedded in the history of late twentieth-century literature and literary criticism. Poststructuralism, we might even say, was fertilized by reformism's corpse—as well as by a drive to unrealizable revolution.

Michel Foucault

Foucault's career reveals him as dancing to the tunes of intellectual fashion—in this he's what Carl Schmitt called a "political romantic"—but also, of course, his career shows him to be a consistently original and revisionist thinker. Despite his persistent enmity to humanism, progressive historicism, and Marxism, there is no single Foucault, especially politically. There's the early literary Foucault who embraced Bataillean transgression; the structuralist, antihistoricist, "archeologist" of *The Order of Things*; the Gaullist technocrat who helped develop the Fouchet reforms of the education system against which the 1968 student movement reacted; the *soixante-huitard* whose genealogies of the disciplinary society and sexuality were researched in the service of gays and prisoners; the post-1968 Foucault who supported Maoist popular justice; and the Foucault of the late 1970s, who became an implicit supporter of neoliberalism. It is this last Foucault I wish briefly to dwell on now.

Foucault's account of neoliberalism is to be found in his 1978–1979 College de France lectures.[3] These were timely, being delivered during the first flush of what Anglophones think of as the Thatcher-Reagan era, which was also the moment when China reconciled itself to capitalism. As such, this moment was an important—if temporary—epoch in endgame capitalism's all but global consolidation. The persona that Foucault adopts in these timely lectures is not that of the organic intellectual (as in his work on discipline), or that of the theorist-poet (as in his structuralist period), or even that of the Nietzschean genealogist releasing subjugated knowledges, but rather that of a neutral historian of present governmentality, that is, of neoliberalism. More concretely, he's concerned to show how neoliberalism became possible when a particular kind of sovereign administration joined a particular modality of rationality or truth. It did so first, he argues, in the work of the so-called German ordoliberals in the 1940s (of whom the most famous is Friedrich Hayek), who proposed new state policies based on classical economic theory not just against Nazi totalitarianism but also against social democracies to come. But ultimately, as Foucault contends, they broke with classical liberalism in Benjamin Constant's or John Stuart Mill's spirit. The ordoliberals produced a new theory of government, indeed of society itself, under whose spell we all now live.

Foucault endorses neoliberalism, if only under cover of neutrality. That's clear if one compares his account to a canonical one that overlaps his own. I am thinking of Karl Polanyi's *The Great Transformation: The Political and Economic Origins of Our Time* (1944), published the same year as Hayek's *The Road to Serfdom* but against its spirit. Polanyi's subtle argument begins with his discovery that the modern concepts of "the economy" and of "society" were both invented in England early in the nineteenth century.[4] The first was developed out of finance capitalism's cosmopolitan efforts to provide international conditions of peace and prosperity, and the second out of the persistence of pauperization under industrialization and the subsequent, politically motivating recognition that market relations damaged community relations. For Polanyi, society is invented as a concept not *for* the economy (as in Foucault) but *against* it. He goes on to argue that "the utopian endeavor of economic liberalism to set up a self-regulating market system" and, especially, a market for labor ultimately led to the Nazi cataclysm not because it is in fact impossible for a self-regulating market system to persist over time but because to allow the economy to order society is to give up on freedom in such a way as to prepare for both Bolshevism and Nazism. Like Foucault, Polanyi is a liberal, but for him liberalism is not a particular mode of governing and being governed but rather is fideistic. It is a "moral and religious" commitment to freedom made in the clear-sighted knowledge that modern society negates both positive and negative freedoms as classical liberalism imagined them (Polanyi 1957, 258). For Polanyi, "uncomplaining acceptance of the reality of society gives man indomitable courage and strength to remove all removable injustice and unfreedom. As long as he is true to his task of creating more abundant freedom for all, he need not fear that either power or planning will turn against him and destroy the freedom he is building by their instrumentality. This is the meaning of freedom in a complex society; it gives us all the certainty that we need" (258). It may have occurred to you that Polanyi's view is not completely removed from the nonprogressivist, simultaneous affirmation of refusal and reform that I am urging here, even if, ascribing to himself something like Job's patience, he replaces refusal by a courageous resignation that offers succor for reformist energies.

But there is almost none of this in Foucault, who treats liberalism's structural tendency to produce what he calls "liberogenic devices," namely antiliberal governmental forms, just as a manageable risk. That's because he regards neoliberalism as a mode of state "self-limitation," a deployment of sovereign power that mandates retreat from itself in order for economic competition and enterprise opportunities to be maximized (Foucault 2008, 69). Foucault's neoliberalism has no enemies or blowback. He has no interest in formal politics: that's the residue of 1968 in him. This also means that there are no feeling, thinking people in his genealogy—no experiences, in short. People are folded into "enterprises": they effectively constitute "human resources" or "human capital" in the now familiar lexicon. But experiences, private or civil, that lie beyond the grasp of economic models cannot be ignored once the machinery of representative democracy enters into governmentality or, indeed, once society is regarded not as an object of government but as civil sociability and interdependency's abstracted web and casing.[5]

And I'd suggest that the avoidance of lived life is exactly what Foucault appears to assent to in neoliberalism. Committed to the aided autonomy and maximization of the market, not only does neoliberalism make no attempt to reform society, except by helping it become more like a market, but, more to the point, it makes no assumptions about, and no attempt to intervene upon, what Foucault calls "anthropology" (that is, the constitutive stuff of human nature) (258–260). Neoliberalism does not normalize. It takes no interest in experience. It rejects rational idealism's concept of duty. Its object and subject is simply the resourceful and enterprising *homo economicus*, a type to whom any personal wants and interests whatever may be granted and whom government empowers by retreating from her social environment (that is, from civil society), so as to provide more opportunities for what Foucault calls "the consumption of freedom." For the neoliberals whom Foucault channels, *homo economicus* is "the abstract ideal, purely economic point that inhabits the dense, full and complex reality of civil society. Or alternatively civil society is the concrete ensemble within which these ideal points must be placed so that they can be appropriately managed" (296). In the end, then, Foucault has (albeit ambiguously) his neoliberal moment because neoliberalism is another form of nonstatist, nonprogressivist nonhumanism that stands outside the reform-revolution problematic brought into being by the modern will to democratic emancipation as occasioned by the continual, often painful, interactions between society and the market.

Antihumanism

Humanism can be defined as the belief that man, not God or nature, lies at the center of history and that history is the path and the measure of human fulfillment. It has strong if finally contingent connections to democracy, since, for humanists, equality, political liberty, and popular sovereignty are characteristically and severally understood as leading to the full extension of human powers and experiences. More particularly, twentieth-century antihumanism often refused democratic state capitalism along two tracks, which are sometimes joined, sometimes not. On one track, it staked a claim that society is reaching a point of collapse that prefigures the unpredictable irruption of an unimaginable new state in which humanity itself would be transformed, usually by returning to its elemental constitution. On the other, it shifted its political (sometimes revolutionary) rejection of social democracy onto other registers, and particularly onto ontology and literature, which thereby became sites for the revelation of the radical incompatibility between modern political and social arrangements and the Being that we fundamentally inhabit. We can immediately note that, in both cases, the test of seriousness is flunked.

One finds the eschatological note first influentially struck, implicitly against imminent democratization, by Nietzsche in *The Birth of Tragedy* (1871), which asserts that the Apollonian mode that has dominated enlightened modernity has overextended itself and that we must now await the imminent return of the Dionysian, conceived as the intoxicated destruction of limits and subjectivity. In effect, it's a form of conservative thought that accepts the stark opposition between revolution and reform and that implies that working for Apollonian reform actually, almost paradoxically, enables revolution—the Dionysian return. And it does so while avoiding practical revolutionary politics. After Heidegger, for whom (in his own phrasing) the retreat of Being heralds Being's reentry, and after 1968 and 1989, when formal communist revolutionary politics ceased to be viable in the West, this Nietzschean politics, headed toward the limitless and unknown, becomes widely accepted in academic "theory." For instance, it organizes even Jean-Luc Nancy's *The Inoperative Community*, which argues against the "myth" of the "passing of the limit," only to replace it with a "literary communism" that aims to undo capitalism by turning us toward "an infinite reserve of common and singular meanings" (Nancy 1991, 77–79). That infinite reserve of singularity that awaits us is ultimately just another form of a nonhumanist, unbounded, and unimaginable community. Radically egalitarian arguments whose roots lie in Maoism, such as Jacques Rancière's, can also be organized inside this logic of nonhumanist eschatology. For instance, Rancière can claim that certain avant-garde literary texts, for example, Mallarmé's, represent "the people to come" (as well as being monuments to that people's absence now), without addressing the question of what historical circumstances might create a community that would indeed be in some—barely imaginable—way *like* Mallarmé's text. This, then, is eschatological thought too: reform and social revolution have both been cast aside.

But it is antihumanism's relation to a revolutionary *reactionary* politics that has touched the literary humanities most profoundly and that does much to explain why reformism has all but been removed from its agenda. This relation takes us quite deep into the historical thickets where interwar European politics intersected with philosophy and intellectual and literary history.

As Stefanos Geroulanos has argued in his recent book *An Atheism That Is Not Humanist Emerges in French Thought*, twentieth-century antihumanism was based on a radicalized "negative anthropology," that is, the idea that man is a *negating* animal as articulated in a widespread rejection of neo-Kantianism, first by Heidegger and then passed on to French thinkers such as Bataille and Blanchot largely via Alexandre Kojève and his "end of history" argument. Instead of the *homo absconditus* that Ernst Bloch was to locate in Karl Barth's and Rudolf Bultmann's "Protestant anthropology" (Bloch 2009, 38–39), we have in this lineage (and talking technically) a "last man," one heir to those "negations" of the world named freedom, history, and individuality, whose historical realization reveals that humanness is ultimately based upon a relation to death.

This philosophic and strategic antihumanism emerges from a looser, larger, older constellation we might call irreligious nonhumanism, by which I mean all those forms of art and thought that were neither religious (in the Judeo-Christian sense) nor humanist, that is, those forms that, while rejecting theism, neither conceived of the human as a value nor thought of history as the gradual and progressive realization of human potential. Such irreligious nonhumanism reaches back into classical antiquity—from this point of view, classicism is *not* a humanism but takes a recognizably modern form after about 1830 in figures (who otherwise may share little) such as Schopenhauer, Stendhal, Flaubert, Thomas Hardy, Henry Adams, Samuel Butler, Georges Sorel, and the post-Catholic Carl Schmitt.[6] At any rate, irreligious nonhumanism is structurally connected to reactionary, anti-Enlightenment antireformism simply because it implies the rejection of progress and, by the same stroke and no less determinedly, the rejection of democracy. This is true even if many irreligious nonhumanists did not identify themselves as conservative at all.

Irreligious nonhumanism first becomes *programmatically* antihumanism in Nietzsche (who declared himself insufficiently Saint-Simonian to "love humanity") as well as in Pierre-Joseph Proudhon, although Proudhon uses the concept of "human dignity" *against* bourgeois liberal and statist humanisms and so can be described as a humanist antihumanist, if one committed to revolution (Proudhon 1887, 25ff.). One particularly revealing moment in the mutation of irreligious nonhumanism into atheist antihumanism occurred in 1911, when T. E. Hulme had a meeting with Pierre Lasserre in Paris. Hulme was then an obscure English critic, attached to A. R. Orage's avant-garde little magazine *New Age*. Hulme was becoming Henri Bergson's leading proselytizer in Britain and would soon translate Sorel's *Reflections on Violence*. He had published the poems that would help define imagism. He was also a polemicist for a new kind of English Toryism removed from nationalist and Anglican monarchism, aligned instead to antiromanticism and to what would later be called "modernism." After Hulme's death in World War I, T. S. Eliot was admiringly and famously to describe him as "classical, reactionary, and revolutionary: he is the antipodes of the eclectic, tolerant, and democratic mind of the last century" (Eliot 1994, 83).

For his part, Lasserre was then Action Française's leading literary intellectual—Action Française being a powerful ultra-rightist movement at the time still loosely allied to the Catholic Church but led by the irreligious Charles Maurras. Formed at a time when democracy was not compulsory and when a refusal of democratic state capitalism appeared to be politically viable, it simultaneously affirmed royalism and popular nationalism against republicanism, socialism, and democracy. It did so under the banners of order, hierarchy, and classical French civilization. In effect, Action Française also detached conservatism from romanticism, as well as from any political theology that interpreted the struggle between revolution and reaction primarily as between Satan and God. But in the end, the movement never solved the problem of how conservative, irreligious nonhumanism might make of itself an effective as well as intellectual force. Although it could mobilize violence on the streets, it never attracted meaningful electoral support. In the end, Maurras himself, a bitter anti-Semite, was jailed for collaboration with the Vichy authorities, having achieved little politically.[7]

Lasserre began his career as a defender of Nietzsche, arguing that Nietzsche was in fact a defender of "civilization" and "*moeurs*," an argument that was to have major implications, some of which we are about to glimpse (Lasserre 1902, 22). Lasserre's Nietzsche is an anti-Rousseau who urges that European civilization is built on nothing like those forms of "mystical democracy" that "attribute to the crowd" a "mysterious power of unconscious creativity both poetic or moral" (54–55). Nor is it built on romantic empathy and imagination. Rather for it—and correctly, according to Lasserre—European civilization is based on the ascetic "work of discrimination, application, and care," a "culture" available only to the aristocracy (24).

At the time that Lasserre met Hulme, the former was most famous for his book on French romanticism, which extended this attack on Rousseau. In *Le romantisme français*, he mounted a strong critique of the postrevolutionary French state for unleashing "social powers" committed to liberal justice but that merely succeeded in pulverizing "the social order," leaving only isolated and unrooted individuals in their wake, doomed to petty egoisms (Lasserre 1908, 346–348). Elaborating on Maurras's key argument that romanticism as established by Rousseau forms the basis of modern revolutionary will and ideology, it also attacked what it called "political pantheism" (or Spinozan immanentism) as romanticism's core tenet. Political pantheism was, Lasserre believed, even more seductive than liberty and equality as a revolutionary principle: it alone could overwhelm experience's resistance to radical change. "Objections carried in the name of experience against the principles of liberty and equality vanish as if under enchantment if a deeper account of reality shows us God present in all individuals," and thence the possibility of emancipating the God in all individuals via a "*magnifique concert spontané*" (393–394). As Hulme himself was to put it in his proto-Orwellian journalese: romanticism fomented the mind-set in which "you don't believe in a God, so you begin to believe that man is a God. You don't believe in Heaven, so you begin to believe in a heaven on earth." This mind-set, therefore, "falsif[ied] and blur[red] the clear outlines of human experience" (Hulme 2004, 62). Within this strand of conservative thought, human experience could be posed against progressivism and reformism. And for it, characteristically, human experience was most lucidly and finely delineated in seventeenth-century literature of the passions, most particularly, for the French, in Racine.

The antihumanism of Hulme, Maurras, and Eliot is important not just because it spreads so far into the literary humanities' antireformism but because it takes us to the border where atheist, reactionary antihumanism, in its search for an institutional base, meets orthodox and reactionary Catholic antihumanism—that is, where it meets the most powerful and venerable of Europe's noncapitalist and nondemocratic institutions. Little illuminates the difficulties of occupying this border than Action Française's contentious relation to Catholicism, which, despite the breadth of the movement's support among French Catholics, would lead to it being formally prohibited by Pope Pius XI in 1926 (the same year, by no coincidence, that T. S. Eliot began his move to Anglo-Catholicism).[8] And I think it likely that the antihumanism that develops in and out of Heidegger and Kojève is also, at certain moments, shaped at this border: one thinks for instance not just of Eliot but of Simone Weil. And it is at this border that orthodox Christianity's refusal to judge any social reformist agenda as finally *serious* (it does not concern the soul, after all) can be transmuted into a formally irreligious antihumanism via a negative anthropology and eschatology (both of which are Judeo-Christian in inspiration) and hence into the advanced academic humanities, where it can push aside the reformist agenda.

In this regard, one must also think of Maurice Blanchot in particular. Blanchot began his career as a journalist in France in the early 1930s on behalf of an anticapitalist, antidemocratic, antiliberal, and anticommunist conservatism, a wholly theoretical conservatism committed above all to revolution. His 1930s ultra-right politics, which he shared with a group of intellectuals sometimes called the "nonconformists" or the "*jeune droite*," emerged out of and around Action Française.[9] Their first manifestos were published in *Reaction* (1931) and *Le Rempart* (1933) and were more fully and radically articulated in the journal *Combat* (1936) and its offshoot, *L'Insurgé*, established the next year, as well as in other more or less short-lived periodicals. Through these channels, Blanchot and his peers radicalized the refusal of democratic capitalism by embracing a revolutionary desire that exceeded the limits of Maurassian order and civilization. Mainly from the safety of their desks, they demanded political action more urgent and extreme than that of Action Française—in the young Blanchot's case by advocating the politics of terror on one occasion at least (Bident 1998, 87ff.). For the young right, as *not* for Action Française, there could be no return to tradition or glory or honor. The concept of civilization was already bankrupt. Revolution was to be carried out not in the name of French culture, custom, and order but in the name of the unimaginable nation or community to come, that is, in the name of Nietzschean eschatology. Blanchot, for instance, met with Maurras's disapproval for arguing on behalf of a "nationalism against the nation" (Montety 1994, 130).

By the mid-1930s, the movement considered the social and political situation under the Popular Front (that is, the condition of democratic state capitalism) to be a disaster: a kind of living death. This was a political diagnosis that in figures like Robert Brasillach could ally itself to fascism, but Blanchot was seduced by neither Hitler nor Mussolini and gradually removed himself from the political scene after 1937. By 1943, he was involved in little except literary criticism and theory. For all that, the Allies' subsequent victory seemed not to have changed Blanchot's ultra-rightist revolutionary politics of refusal at a deep level. It is as if, for him, postwar social democracy preserved the social disaster and abasement of the Popular Front era, but now without hope. History's end had come in the victorious alliance between the Bolshevik and democratic-capitalist states, which had allowed both polities to survive into the postwar era, an alliance that prefigured what conservatives of the time were prophetically naming a "totalitarian democracy," as we will see in the next chapter. At any rate, Blanchot came to accept a darkly Heideggerian version of Kojève's end-of-history thesis.

Except for the decade between 1958 and 1968, when he became involved in ultra-leftist politics against Gaullism, Blanchot ceased to engage in politics as such, becoming instead one of France's most respected and innovative critics and fiction writers. His criticism, published with unremitting regularity in the most prestigious journals, was developed in exchange with a series of predecessors and contemporaries (Bataille, Levinas, Barthes, Derrida, Nancy) but also with Kafka and Beckett. As such, it became nodal, inserting itself into the thought of figures as different from one another as Barthes, Foucault, de Man, Deleuze, and Derrida, so as to help energize what would become anti- or at least nonreformist "poststructuralism" in the Anglophone academy. The terms of that passage from Blanchot to poststructuralism are conceptually difficult but not obscure: they are spelled out both by Blanchot himself in his account of Foucault's antihumanism in *The Order of Things* and by Foucault in his essay on Blanchot, where he establishes a genealogy that links early Christian mysticism to poststructuralism's "breakthrough to a language from which the subject is excluded," via Blanchot's (and Bataille's) concept of "experience" (see Blanchot 1993, 246–263; and Foucault 1994, 1:518–539; see also Nancy 2005, 129ff.).

Blanchot's basic move is to displace the conceptual structure of his ultraright, antireformist, revolutionary refusal of democratic capitalism onto literature. In effect, when he gives up on nationalism, he transforms his image of the nation under social democracy into a theory of literature or literary space itself.[10] To use Blanchot's own title to his inaugural contribution to *L'Insurgé*, he moved "from revolution to literature," and it's by virtue of that shift that he reconfigured what we might call literary ontology (Blanchot 1937). Now, it is literature that expresses the interminability of bare existence (the Neutral, the *il y a*) and that takes the form of a debased, diseased natural law. Now, it is literature that is a mode of refusal and that is written from and for disaster. Now, it is literature that is inhabited by and appropriates death, to use a phrase that Blanchot applied to Maurras in 1937, if a death that no longer marks life's end (cited in Verdès-Leroux 1996, 86).

It's useful to substantiate this argument by examining two particular moments in Blanchot's passage from a revolutionary denunciation of democratic capitalism to the construction of a new theory of literature, in part because they provide an entry point for analyses in later chapters. The first is Georges Bataille's *Inner Experience* (1943), a work, written under the Vichy regime, that brings mysticism into contact with (post-)Nietzschean nihilism. It is relevant here mainly because Blanchot contributed important arguments to the book (as Bataille repeatedly acknowledges) and also because it is itself an important document in the history of the theorization of democratic experience.

Bataille argues for the centrality of an "experience" of ecstatic torment, which lies outside all use-value, all representation, all justification, all efforts at relief from pain—all "projects," as he puts it, in an implicit reference to Heidegger. In a sense, he is attempting "to realize the character of experience absolutely," as Michael Oakeshott defined philosophy's task in 1933 (Oakeshott 1933, 328). But Bataille's inner experience is not really an experience at all in the Deweyian sense. Rather, it is a "voyage to the end of the possible of man" (Bataille 1988, 7). It is a recognizably Dionysian encounter with anthropological limits that happens and communicates through dramatization, laughter, silence, and, importantly, writing, inside an obscure solitude, an interruption of intersubjectivity, which, however, is not attached merely to individuals. Inner experience is also an ontological contestation—a contestation of what is, which allows for an "expiation" of authority's necessity—these being the concepts that Blanchot provided to Bataille for the book and that suggest inner experience's capacity to atone for, but not wholly repudiate, the horrors caused by the radical conservative war against democracy. In short, the book's strategy of refusal (which is also a retreat into interiority if not into individuality) ruptures the concept of experience itself. In doing so, it offers a promise that is both eschatological and literary just because, for both Bataille and Blanchot, inner experience and writing are so closely bound to each other. For them, writing is the practice through which contestatory, deindividuating inner experience is realized.

The passage from the refusal of humanist social democracy to literary theory is clearer still in another, more limited instance—in the ultra-right's reception of the great seventeenth-century dramatist Racine. For this group, Racine was not just a canonical writer but a shibboleth, a test of faith. That became true after 1910, when the Camelots du Roi—the (mainly student) newspaper hawkers for Action Française's periodicals who also worked as bodyguards and stormtroopers at demonstrations—rioted against a lecture on the playwright by René Fauchois. Fauchois, a popular actor and dramatist, complained that Racine was dull and outdated. Fauchois himself (for what it's worth) was to write the play upon which Jean Renoir based his *Boudu Saved from Drowning* and thus is the distant progenitor of the Hollywood movie *Down and Out in Beverly Hills*. The postwar radical conservatives' very different reading of Racine was spelled out in Thierry Maulnier's *Racine* (1935) and *Lecture de Phèdre* (1943), books that have been republished innumerable times and remain in print in France to this day.

Maulnier, a critic, journalist, and political theorist and one of Action Française's leading second-generation intellectuals, argues, like Lasserre, for an understanding of French classicism that can be reconciled to Nietzsche as well as mobilized for the new forms of radical (and Sorelian) conservatism.[11] His early book on Nietzsche, for instance, presents a figure whose commitment to the Dionysian future, wholly against the spirit of the time, goes so far as to make him "his own hangman" (Maulnier 1925, 226). Maulnier reinterprets Nietzsche's heroic refusal of modernity as a cult of individual sacrifice to the community to come (222ff.).

Maulnier's *Racine* also reveals human life's violence and horror. He elucidates "*le jour de la catastrophe et de la mort*" (Maulnier 1947, 18). And he reveals that that catastrophe is *fated*. It follows that Racine's classicist formalism, his obedience to Aristotelian rules, is not to be considered as a "constraint" but rather as a literary technique for representing fatedness, once more as a formal expression of a primordial will to sacrifice and loss. Maulnier generalizes and politicizes this insight: Racine shows that what the "stupid adorers of French clarity and order" (27) suppose classicism to be is exactly what it is not. It is not "the application of a learnt technique which refers to masters, schools and predecessors." It is not a straitjacketing of "primitive inspiration." It is not a moment in which Apollo dominates Dionysius. Rather, it is an assimilation of order by instinct, "an atavistic conjuration between perfection and spontaneity" (26), implicitly available to inspire opportunistic uprisings against the social democratic order.

Written during the Vichy regime, Maulnier's next book on Racine, *Lecture de Phèdre*, subtly changes tack. Racine is still the "poet of night," and in *Phèdre* this darkness thickens. Upon the play's completion, Racine will write no more tragedies. He becomes silent. Why? On one level, Maulnier contends that it was because he could no longer reconcile "church" and "theatre" (Maulnier 1943, 27). But more profoundly, it was because he reached the point where his work exceeded his own creative will and the whole worldly machinery of "ordinary life" and of "education and edification" (150). The work is an expression of what is "dark, rebellious, unknown, inaccessible," and "uncontainable" (152). Under the compulsion of a "professed necessity," Racine has written a play that he could neither control nor intend, a work that "abolishes the judges" and that, "impure and terrible," commits itself to the "fascination of perdition" (158). By opening the doors of an art that is "too dangerous," he reaches the "limits of his technique and courage" (162). Racine is the poet who reaches the limits of human possibility, who takes experience out of the mundane and toward his own kind of Blanchotian/Bataillean inner experience.

Such a reading clearly displaces the pathos of the ultra-rightist project's collapse, its abjection under Vichy and its ambiguous relation to the war that was about to be lost, onto Racine's classical tragedy. And it is at this point that Blanchot enters again.[12] He reviewed Maulnier's second book on Racine immediately on its publication, Maulnier being perhaps the person to whom Blanchot had been most closely ideologically attached during his first years as a Parisian journalist. The review is little more than a condensation of Maulnier's argument, although it lays more stress on Phaedra's divided self—her split between an incestuous desire for Hippolytus and a love of purity and innocence, which carries her toward Theseus. But in Blanchot's plangent prose, Maulnier's argument points forward to a waiting future as well as back to the catastrophe of the late 1930s. Those arguments remain expressions simultaneously of the affirmation and undoing of a dark, Nietzschean classicism. But there's also a sense of a new understanding that Racinean/Nietzschean classicism (as understood by Maulnier) *must*, paradoxically, be defeated by democracy, because defeat seals its contestation. Defeat protects tragic, Dionysian rebelliousness.

This is to begin to broach the more extreme and general notion that Blanchot would come to in his postwar writings, namely that in democracy (which for Blanchot inherits the remorseless transparency and confidence of revolutionary terror), literature itself proceeds under the sign of defeat. Democracy is radically inhospitable to literature. It makes literature in effect unreadable, because literature can allow us to experience anything at all by virtue of its power to create the new and other and so to annihilate the world that we have. Structurally, therefore, literature is endlessly pointed beyond life, transparency, community, and history toward groundlessness, destruction, and death. These are terms on which it takes experience beyond society's, and especially democratic society's, grasp. But, as Blanchot came to believe, democracy's indifference to literature and its life fulfills that "right to death" in which literature can properly be itself.

In slightly different terms, it is as if Blanchot chooses the other side of Pascal's wager. He makes a bet against God, a bet that the world is not just immanent and Godless but "catastrophic." That's a wager that can't pay out—it's staked in a kind of madness—except insofar as it rescues you, if not exactly from atheism, then from mundanity. At this point, maybe "atheist antihumanism" can be conceived of as positioned against ordinary social being—the very hope of hope. It mutates what I've been calling emptied social hope into an ontological claim whose genealogy belongs to radical conservatism and that, under political pressure, can be ascribed to literary writing now imagined as leading to a frozen, dark *kairos*.

After the war, Blanchot attempted to work out a practice of life that was maximally *in* the literary so conceived. This helped him to accrue glamour to an extent where it became possible to say, as Foucault did in 1966, that it was he "who has made all discourse on literature possible" (Foucault 1996, 22). Blanchot turned to politics only under de Gaulle's Fifth Republic, when revolutionary possibilities flickered again for him. (His switch from the ultra-right to the ultra-left, which placed him on the other side politically of his old colleague Maulnier, is exemplary not so much because it reveals structural equivalences between the two positions but because it reveals that the conservative/progressivist opposition is minimized once democratic state capitalism has been refused.) At any rate, Blanchot avoided the bicameral structure of simultaneously refusing and engaging the social world in favor of a reformulated concept of literature as the positive expression of destitution, the grounds of refusal. And precisely because of the richness of his politicohistorical trajectory, Blanchot represents, possibly better than anyone else, the strange logic by which refusal, nursed in the history of antidemocracy and counter-Enlightenment, trumped reformism in the world of avant-garde literature and theory, in part just because reformism trumped refusal in the larger world. But of course, what happens to refusal in this structure—a refusal displaced onto the literary—is that it is *practically* indistinguishable from assent in the sense that it makes no actual political difference and cannot enter into a relation with policy formation and implementation. It's not serious.

THREE

Conservatism and Critique

Certain historical moments prophetically illuminate the future. One such moment occurred during the dark early days of World War II in Britain, when it seemed as if Nazi Germany were about to defeat Western liberal democracy. It was at this moment that the concept "totalitarian democracy" was invented, a term that seems to have been first used by the conservative Catholic political theorist Christopher Dawson. Extending a line of thought earlier propounded in Hilaire Belloc's *The Servile State* (1912), Dawson argued that totalitarianism (of which he was by no means an automatic enemy) might result from the democratic state's increasing control and socialization of the capitalist mode of production (Dawson 1939, 83–84). A similar position was then taken up by T. S. Eliot in his 1939 pamphlet *The Idea of a Christian Society* to describe how liberalism can "prepare the way for its own negation" by requiring forms of "artificial, mechanized or brutalized control" in order to remedy the social chaos and distress that liberalism causes (Eliot 1960, 12). At the time, George Orwell was also arguing that, as the state and capitalism were reconciled in Europe, freedom and autonomy thought of in the classical mode, both already very faded, were likely to disappear altogether (Orwell 1968, 134). From a very different perspective, Friedrich Hayek agreed. In the first few pages of *The Road to Serfdom* (Hayek 1944, 2), he claimed that if democratic statism were left unchecked among the nations who were fighting Hitler, they would be in danger of repeating Germany's fate.

But the basic structures of totalitarian democracy were spelled out in greater detail in an essay that, in taking the concept of totalitarian democracy further, doesn't actually use the name. In his 1941 lecture "Diagnosis of the Time," Karl Mannheim argued that regardless of who won the war—the democrats or the fascists—Europe was headed toward a new kind of "planned" society, one characterized by an unprecedentedly high degree of state control and an unprecedentedly high share of total productive activity (including cultural activity) based in large, "planned," private corporations. Mannheim recognized that modern state capitalism could only function smoothly (if at all) if managed nondemocratically by experts and bureaucrats continually fiddling and fine-tuning economic and social policy settings and levers. For Mannheim, such a society would involve new levels of centralization. And that led him to conclude that the main policy problems to be dealt with by what he called "planning for freedom" was to enable the state's experts to retrain citizens to develop their capacities to evaluate, experience, and assent to the new society and to assess the degree to which the state might "refrain" from intervening in civil society (Mannheim 1943, 10–11, 21–22).

The Allies' victory over the Nazis sidelined this rather bleak vision or, at any rate, mutated it into a more obviously progressive understanding of Western postwar societies as developed social democracies. But it's fair to say that since the delegitimization of socialism after about 1968, and also as a result of the increasingly tight integration of state administration, the political system, the market, and the media that I invoked in Chapter 1, "totalitarian democracy" has come to seem just about as accurate a description of contemporary social organization as, say, "social democracy." Recent analyses as different as those by Sheldon Wolin, Jacques Attali, Raymond Geuss, and Wendy Brown all point in that direction, insofar as they suggest that the current democratic polity is marked by systemic failures because it has become possible for decentralization to occur simultaneously with far-reaching erosion of autonomies, both institutional and private, as well as with the concentration of power in a state-market nexus.[1]

As we have seen, the totalizing reach of existing governmental structures has become stronger since the 1940s for ideological reasons, too. After all, there is a sense in which *compulsory* democracy is, all by itself, totalitarian democracy. And, of course, compulsory democracy is—more or less contingently—bound to compulsory capitalism, just because today it appears that only a society grounded in private property, market relations, and highly developed financial instruments can support national economies that are sufficiently strong to retain their citizens' full support and trust.[2] It is these strict ideological limits that mean that the present moment implicitly imagines itself as having completed the historical journey toward the best possible governmental and distribution system, despite the system's clear insufficiencies.

Obviously enough, this retrieval of a 1940s European frame of mind repeats the broad sweep of my own argument as outlined in chapter 1, and it led me in the previous chapter to argue for the simultaneous affirmation of social refusal and social reform. But in the 1940s, an alternative mode of intellectual resistance to totalitarian democracy seemed possible to a few theorists. This mode of intellectual resistance was called "critique," an old name for a new thing.

We can define modern critique succinctly as reason applied against constitutive social unreason, where "constitutive social unreason" refers approximately to the systemic social failures that we have classified earlier as distributional, administrative, and experiential.[3] As a concept, critique has its origin in Kantian philosophy, at least to the degree that it too is committed to the notion that rationality must be ethically and epistemologically autonomous (that is, must be independent of any particular ontology or experience). Society fails where it is unable to protect a form of individual freedom that is itself only available through that kind of independent, rational action. It fails, then, for Kantianism when people are not treated as ends in and for themselves. In the dog days of the late 1930s and the 1940s, seeking ways out of the reform/revolution polarity (and with a strong intuition of totalitarian democracy to come), the Frankfurt School politicized critique as conceived within this lineage. In Max Horkheimer's definitive 1937 essay "Traditional and Critical Theory," for instance, critique clearly still belongs to enlightened (universal and autonomous) rationalism and is understood as critical *theory* precisely because it is not seconded to experience, experience being too concrete and too socially embedded to provide the grounds for a critical conspectus on history and society.[4] Yet although modern critique retains a connection to its Kantian heritage, it is nonetheless immanent and situational. It takes into account the ways in which reason has itself become a tool for the domination of both nature and people, it takes into account the ways in which reason can be used to legitimate callous policy and systems, and it takes into account the fact that individuals can be thought of as free and autonomous only within idealism. In sum, it takes into account reason's indifference to experiential substance, to the particularity of particular cases and situations. So it does not bring absolute ideas of morality or justice to bear on particular cases and conditions; rather, its philosophical analyses are developed, almost casuistically, within and against specific situations, whether evanescent and local or deeply seated and general, calling upon inherited categories of thought to reveal the deeper structures that organize immediate conditions and conflicts characteristically in order to overcome subjectivism and instrumentalism, on the one side, and the "bourgeois" understanding of the workings of society as beyond the control of human agencies, on the other (Horkheimer 1972, 189–190). As such, it knows that, despite everything, it itself belongs to those modernizing processes of rationalization that, however, it wishes to deflect toward substantive freedom and justice.

Nonetheless, critique in this mode, which refuses refusal, may serve revolution as easily as reformism, even if it remains detached from any active proletarian/communist party and even if revolution has become unimaginably remote. By wresting reason back from capitalist instrumentality; by introducing totalities (the context of the whole) only graspable theoretically to adjudicate particular conditions; and by insisting that individuals' intuitions, experiences, and beliefs are mediated socially, critique tells the (revolutionary) truth about society without accepting immediate responsibility for working toward change (220–221). For that reason, it belongs in particular to intellectuals. That it also thus fails the seriousness test is irrelevant from this perspective, since truth-telling and actual reformist or revolutionary agency remain distinct from each other or at any rate are different kinds of "praxis." Even if critique isn't itself serious in the requisite sense (it doesn't practically help toward change), it does, so the argument goes, provide us with the theoretical knowledge that we need to grasp the truth of those situations under which critical intellectuals can become seriously engaged in working toward revolutionary transformation.

Today, the politics that generated Horkheimer's concept and practice of critique have, of course, disappeared. Revolution has been removed from the table. Reform is repositioned as the dual management of the distribution of national prosperity and of modernity's damage to itself. Democracy is compulsory. So is capitalism. The notion of the social whole is all but meaningless in a system whose borders are so open and that so thoroughly and effectively joins integration to fragmentation. No less important, the philosophical underpinnings of critique have been undermined, too. As Adorno wrote, "It hearkens back to the philosophical tradition that today lies in ruins" (Adorno 1998, 7). In particular, critique's rootedness in the Kantian categories of reason dates it. Between them, empiricism, positivism, and pragmatism—capitalist democracy's intellectual godparents and its handmaidens, too—have pushed that kind of reason into retreat. Today, when rationalist philosophers embark on a task somewhat like critique—I am thinking of figures as different as John Rawls and Alain Badiou—then they are compelled to elaborate their own philosophical systems in ways that shift the balance between philosophy and social criticism to the former's advantage. Rawls and Badiou are important not for what they tell us about society or for how they help us change it but for what they tell us about current possibilities for the application of philosophic reason. That was less true of the Frankfurt School, which, as Adorno made clear in the 1960s in his lectures on negative dialectics, aimed to "demonstrate the power" of the philosophical energy previously geared to building rational systems, so as "to blast open individual phenomena through the insistent power of thought," that is, to deploy critique's power against society's power to abstract, misrecognize, and destroy (Adorno 2008, 40).

If critique in this lineage has become impossible in part because of democratic state capitalism's insurmountability, that's also because in it, critique can no longer appeal in particular to democracy or democratization as a norm or telos. After all, today, any call to further democratize or to redemocratize state capitalism in the era of compulsory democracy is, in the end, a call to intensify or solidify the regime that we have. That is true even if we radically reformulate democracy—even if we believe, as Jacques Rancière does, for instance, that true democracy must break out of the machinery of representation and party politics and return to direct democracy or to the election of governmental officials by lottery. Or if we believe, like John Keane, that the Internet's capacity to inspect and denounce government and corporate abuse (so-called monitory democracy) might effectively supplement popular sovereignty. Or if we believe that the democratization of control over capitalist business institutions (whether corporate boards or hired workforces) can allow us to resist the market's full capacity for creative destruction. But such gestures toward better or different democracies still remain inside the conceptual framework that legitimates the system. The moment when new democratic forms or agencies will become viable, if that moment ever comes, will be the moment when they can help strengthen democratic state capitalism.

Rather—and this is my argument—what stands in the place of critique must now be based on those moments, traditions, concepts, and institutions in which democracy and capitalism have, directly or indirectly, been judged and rejected, or at least resisted, *in the past*. My invocation of perfection as a ground of hope and judgment in the previous chapter was itself an example of such a backward turn, a nonmodern concept that tribunalizes (to use Odo Marquard's useful term) the modern order. And so was modern literary criticism itself in its founding moment, as I shall argue in the next chapter. To think like this is not necessarily to invoke some disappeared golden age. Without jeopardizing the logic of this turn, we can, if we like, think of the impact of democratic state capitalism on society pessimistically as the further ruination of ruins or more positively as the best system we can imagine but still not good enough. But—here is the crux—this appeal to the past against the present in the future's interest will, necessarily, belong to what we have thought of as conservatism. Conservatism happens, then, whenever the past tribunalizes the present and, by the same stroke, when a check to progressivism is administered. What remains of strong critical thought outside the reform/refusal division—in other words, what remains of critique—today is *in* conservatism conceived of like this, but, crucially, this is a conservatism that has almost nothing in common with those political groupings who call themselves conservative. Otherwise put: leftist progressivism having become, willy-nilly, an arm of social democratic state capitalism, substantive negation of the system is, it would seem, being transferred to conservatism. In the same moment, critique becomes a mode of awaiting the past, under whatever guise (cf. Blanchot 1986).

At this point, we strike a practical difficulty. Conservatism remains undertheorized. It has been so delegitimized in the academic humanities since 1945, or at least since the 1968 emancipation movements, that it has become all but invisible among us, despite some illuminating scholarship.[5] Those whose work is indeed conservative (Charles Taylor, Alasdair MacIntyre, radical orthodoxy) usually downplay that fact. In this context, it is worth recalling that Adorno and Walter Benjamin can already be thought of as radically conservative thinkers as easily as progressive ones. If it comes to that, in an ambitious, program-outlining 1843 letter to Arnold Ruge, the young Marx himself could declare, hitting a note that radically breaks with radicalism and joins a certain conservatism, "our task is not to draw a sharp mental line between past and future but to complete the thought of the past . . . it will become plain that mankind will not begin any *new* work, but will consciously bring about completion of its old work" (Marx 1985, 209). Yet today it's all but impossible for an academic in the humanities to say "I am a conservative"—I don't say that myself, and anyone who thinks that this book implicitly makes such a statement will have misunderstood it. Probably the last widely known consciously conservative intervention on debates in the humanities was Allan Bloom's *The Closing of the American Mind*, published in 1987, an intemperate and uncomprehending denunciation of pluralism and relativism in the spirit of Leo Strauss's 1960s essays on the liberal humanities, which did conservatism no service at all.

In fact, it is in the prewar period that we can find the careful and sympathetic accounts of conservatism that are most useful to those of us today whose interest is primarily in culture and literature. One of the strongest analyses remains Karl Mannheim's doctoral dissertation *Conservatism: A Contribution to the Sociology of Knowledge*, whose first version dates as far back as 1917, where it appeared out of that exciting pre–World War I Budapest intellectual scene that collected around the young György Lukács and the Polanyi brothers (Michael and Karl), and that, by virtue of its relation to Lukács, also had a formative relation to Adorno's and Horkheimer's thoughts of the 1930s and 1940s. I want to begin to develop my brief account of conservatism here by offering a summary of Mannheim's thesis and then go on to inquire into a book in dialogue with it—Carl Schmitt's *Political Romanticism* (first edition 1919, second revised edition 1925)—before returning the analysis to the problem of contemporary "critique" in the academic humanities.

First, it is important to clarify conservatism's conceptual structure. Let me do so in summary form.

1. Conservatism is a diffuse formation that exists both in a programmatic and in a latent or unformulated mode. Programmatic conservatism knows and names itself as conservative. Latent conservatism (small "c" conservatism) does not, even though it too resists or stands against the organized processes or normative grounds of progressive change. Latent conservatism is indeed embedded across the array of dispositions available to us in ordinary life, since it seems very difficult, even across cultures, not to succumb to its most basic and habitual mode, that is, the turning of memories and inheritances into models or lessons.

2. In its modern and programmatic mode at least, conservatism is reactive. I do not here cavil with Mannheim's conventional argument that modern political conservatism begins in the reaction against the 1789 French revolutionary ideals and in particular against liberty and equality. This itself marks conservatism as diffuse, since liberty and equality appeal to different principles and in practice may contradict each other, as is well known and as we will see further in the next chapter.

3. Conservatism may be diffuse, but it contains distinct genres distinguished by different theoretical presuppositions. Some of the more important are:

i. Ultraconservatism (which in fact predates modern conservatism) argues that human social order depends ultimately on (a Christian orthodox understanding of) God's absolute sovereignty of the world. For it, human sovereignty, at whatever level, mimics divine sovereignty.
ii. Hobbesian conservatism argues that society can only be stable where sovereign authority is unquestionable but that this authority is ultimately based on (a myth of) originary consent by individuals in a state of nature. Modern versions of Hobbesian conservatism include Michael Oakeshott's argument that a strong central state ("parliamentary sovereignty") is required to protect government from being overwhelmed by the interests of private associations.
iii. Burkean conservatism contends that inherited community practices and forms ("culture") possess an inherent value and stability that cannot be respected by any progressivism that attempts to impose abstract, purely rational norms on received institutions.
iv. De Maistrean conservatism argues that progressivism and democratization cannot be adequate forms of government since they cannot manage

man's sinful or fallen nature. This form of conservatism can take a Nietzschean turn, as we have seen in Maulnier, Bataille, and Blanchot, for whom Joseph de Maistre's notion of Christian sin is replaced by a concept of tragedy or, more radically, by a Dionysian will to the ecstatic and catastrophic breaking of limits.

v. Straussian conservatism argues that progressivism depends on a historicism that fails to reconcile itself to the fundamentally limited, ahistorical (and hierarchical) structures of civil and intellectual (and natural) life and, in particular, to the unique human importance of philosophic thought about the purpose and ends of the good life, thought that will remain limited to an elite and is thence "esoteric," that is, cannot be communicated widely across society, since it is ultimately subversive of order.

vi. Naturalist conservatism argues that human talents are hierarchized as anthropological fact and that both justice as desert and social order demand that this hierarchy be reflected in society's organization. In naturalizing inequality, this form of conservatism hearkens back to those nonmodern natural-law theories that pictured the world as a ranked "chain of being."

4. For all that, conservatism is a relative formation. Particular ideas or values are not conservative by nature; they are conservative as historically situated and intended. This means that what is not conservative in one historical moment may be conservative in another. The most obvious example would be those forms of liberalism that were progressive before about 1848, but after 1848, when the working class appeared on the scene as a self-identified political agent armed with socialism as a political philosophy, liberalism became "conservative" because it was resistant to the forces of progress as then understood by socialism. (And since that time, many forms of conservatism have indeed absorbed elements of liberalism.) What limits conservatism's relativism is its structural tendency to support hegemony. But conservatism certainly does not simply name the intellectual formations that work in the interest of ruling classes at any particular moment, since radical forms of conservative dissent are always available. One thinks, for instance, of Europe's various revolutionary ultra-rightisms in the 1920s and 1930s, as discussed above.

5. Conservatism is ineluctable. If it is all but impossible for contemporary humanities academics to say "I am a conservative," it is also very difficult for them in fact to stand outside conservatism's genealogies. To take a

hard case, this is even true of Rancière's thought, which one might suppose to be as remote from conservatism as possible. It's not just that his notion of radical democracy contains memories of Athenian democracy. He too sometimes affirms "a structure of collective life wrested from the sole reign on the law of private interest, and the imposition of limits on the naturally limitless process of the increase of wealth" (Rancière 2006, 57), which, like all communitarianisms, belongs as much to a certain strand of conservative thought as it does to leftism—it's a sentiment that G. K. Chesterton, for instance, would have endorsed. And what is true for communitarianism is also true, if more weakly, for all associationalisms, even leftist ones, including those in Antonio Gramsci's slipstream, which argue the case for strategic alliances between heterogeneous groups in the interests of politically enacted radical change. That's because this kind of thinking belongs to the tradition that pits civil society against established political institutions, whether as a saving supplement, resistant force, or externality—a local, situational, "disincarnated" democracy outside the "abstraction" of the state, as Simon Critchley puts it (Critchley 2007, 117)—and that tradition, which notably includes Tocqueville, maintains a suspicion of regulated, formal, rational, consensual, "abstract" administrative apparatuses that is indelibly conservative, if sometimes liberal or anarchic or revolutionary as well. And this is so even if *another* conservatism (Oakeshott's, for instance) wishes to empower the state against civil associations. So there are two broad reasons for conservatism's inescapability. First, just because it is so diffuse, relative, and various, and just because it is so easy (I want to say "natural") to use the past to judge the present, few political projects and ideas have not been situated within it at one time or another, with the demand for substantive individual equality in society being perhaps an exception. And even a temporary habitation of conservatism leaves its traces on a particular idea or value; it stamps it as a reserve for the critique of, or resistance to, purposive enlightened modernization. Second, as soon as content is given to the ends of reform, revolution, or modernization, then conservatism makes an entry, since it has become impossible to imagine a good society-to-come except by reference to idealized good societies-that-have-been.

Now to Karl Mannheim's *Conservatism*, as a text that can help us recognize certain basic stakes in the task of reformulating radical thought under compulsory democracy.

I have already accepted Mannheim's thesis that modern conservatism is primarily to be considered as a reaction to emancipation movements unleashed by the French Revolution. More particularly, Mannheim, writing inside the German-dominated academy around the period of World War I, regarded progressivism as a mode of neo-Kantianism. For him, progressivism is based on a Kantian separation of "is" and "ought," history being regarded as the trajectory and, since the Enlightenment, the purposive trajectory toward a freedom conceived of as the realization of rational, universal sociopolitical principles (or what Mannheim himself calls "natural law"; Mannheim 1997, 37). So it is also based on a Kantian ideal of the individual subject, not just as fundamentally autonomous and committed to universal freedom via reason but as unified and disembodied. Mannheim attaches this philosophical understanding of progress to a sociological one along Weberian lines, in which historical progress is thought of as the gradual attainment of the high degree of integration, functionalization, and specialization that orders the contemporary global market-state system. Furthermore, in practice, progressivism is embraced by that class whom modernization benefits most: the bourgeoisie.

In a Marxian spirit, Mannheim also argues that in postrevolutionary capitalist society, constituted around class struggles through which the state and market steadily encroach on old lifeways, experience itself becomes politicized. In particular, under the spell of its rational, universal, and transcendental teleology, bourgeois experience (or, as we might also say, subjectivity) acquires a specific quality. It is directed toward the secular future; it is calculating and manipulative.

> Our attitude towards things, persons and institutions is different . . . at the level of experience (*Erleben*), when we view them from some standpoint of how they "ought" to be from what it is when we accept them as "something which has grown" or as an "existent" which has become necessary. The effect of the former of these attitudes is that we will never do more than to glance off the world around us: we do not bring it a forgiving love, and we lack the interest in its existence which would arise from solidarity with it. (9)

We may be surprised to recognize a Christian—indeed a Thomist—spirit in phrases like "forgiving love" here, but Mannheim's perspective remains secular. Hence he names romanticism as that mode of experience that stands *against* bourgeois experience and in solidarity with the world.

(It is worth noticing in passing that Mannheim's account of romanticism's political purposes is pretty much the opposite of that offered by T. S. Eliot and the Maurrassians.) And, for Mannheim, romanticism, at least as it emerged in Germany around 1800, characteristically "approaches the particular from behind, from the past" (96). That is, romanticism is historicist just because in the modern era "history . . . takes the place of divine transcendence" (56). This analysis is the springboard from which Mannheim mounts some ambitious claims. First, that romanticism is precisely a conservatism. Second, that, because it is sensitive to the richness of the present and Being as such, conservative romanticism is invested in the concrete, not in the abstract. Third, that it affirms quality rather than quantity as a criterion of worth. Fourth, conservative romanticism is communitarian and does not advance autonomization.

Most of all, romanticism tends toward a *Lebensphilosophie* whose latest guise in the 1910s and 1920s was to be found in Dilthey's and Bergson's work, as it is to be found in Deleuze in our own time. Mannheim's evocation of *Lebensphilosophie* from this perspective is worth citing at length:

> However much the tendencies within "philosophy of life" may differ from one another, they nevertheless all betray their origin in romanticism and counter-revolution by *their common opposition to Kantianism as well as to positivism*, the two variants of bourgeois rationalizing thinking which both endeavor to uphold universal concepts and the natural-scientific, generalizing mode of thought. . . . All these varied philosophies of life are at root romantic because the common position against generalizing concepts survives in them and they seek for the truly real in *pure experience* (*reinen Erlebnis*), phenomenologically freed from conceptualized models and not screened by reason. . . .
>
> The great significance of this philosophy of life lies in its constant emphasis on the abstractness of bourgeois rationalism, whose expansion gradually threatens to cover over (to "reify") all elements of life. It steadily points out that the world of relations which we experience in a rationalized world are actually rational relations which have been absolutized into a "fetish," in other words, that this allegedly real world is nothing but the world of capitalist rationalization which covers over a world of underlying "pure experience." The conservative origin of this current still betrays itself today, however, in the fact that it is an inactive opposition to the rationalized world which surrounds us. Because it is depoliticized in the widest sense of the term, it cannot find the direct way to change. It has inwardly given up on the world which is in the state of

> becoming (if only along rationalized lines). But . . . it serves to keep alive a germ of experience (*einen Erlebniskeim*) . . . it teaches us again and again to dismantle (*abzubauen*) the rationalizations which conceal the real nature of things and to avoid orienting consciousness to the real of the theoretical attitude alone. It is always showing that the "reasonable" ("*Vernunftmässige*") and "objectified" are relative and partial. (150–151)

This passage, clearly inspired by Lukács, begins to preempt the Frankfurt School's critique of the Enlightenment for conservatism. It also attends to what's at stake in naming intellectual lineages or continuities "conservative" (or "romantic") past the point at which they have lost their programmatic charge, that is, have become depoliticized. On the one side, antirationalizing (which is to say, anticapitalist, antimodernizing) currents, those which, to use a formula, deliver themselves to a solidarity with Being rather than to reformist change, tend to "give up on the world" in what is itself a conservative gesture. Mannheim himself considers the turn to pure experience as retreat more than as resistance, which explains why it so often inclines toward the "theological-mystical" (he may have in mind Bergson, who tended toward mysticism as he grew older). At any rate, he has little sense here of what will become a truism inside a strand of conservative thought, especially Benjamin's, namely that democratic capitalism develops and expands so quickly and complexly that its subjects lose the capability to translate social reality into transmissible experiences at all. By ignoring the problematic of experiential inadequacy, Mannheim can claim that the turn to Being against modernization may "serve to keep alive a germ of experience" in hard times, a germ of resistant experience that will be available to be reconnected and recombined into new political programs. And we should add that, while this germ remains fundamentally conservative, these programs might belong either to the left or to the right in the world of practical politics.

To anticipate my argument a little, and to overlook Mannheim's optimism about subject formation, this line of thought would mean that the academic humanities, insofar as they too conserve experiences of the world that oppose and stand outside technologico-Benthamitism, as F. R. Leavis famously called it, can themselves be regarded as conservative storehouses for resistances to come.

Let me now move toward Schmitt's *Political Romanticism*, which can be read as a riposte to Mannheim's argument. Mannheim had contended that since the eighteenth century intellectuals had both become detached from established social castes (they had become "free-floating," as he was later famously to say) and at the same time bearers of *Geist*'s "destiny" (119). This meant that intellectual life was in the carriage of weak vessels. In the German romantic period at least, intellectuals attempted to solve the problem of their situation of simultaneous weakness and power by encouraging dispositions—or practices of self—that heighten mundane experiences and activities. To this end, Mannheim cites a well-known passage from Novalis: romantics were intent on "giving an exalted meaning to the vulgar, a mysterious aspect to the commonplace, the dignity of the unknown to the familiar, the semblance of infinity to the finite" (120). But at the same time, the romantics rediscovered a prerevolutionary understanding of the social in what Mannheim called "the thoughts of the old estates," namely those modes of preabsolutist corporatist thinking in which different and independent castes and corporations, joined together to constitute the commonwealth, were the main agents in social and political negotiation and deliberation. Mannheim argued that in an estatist constitution, the criteria for action and judgment were fundamentally phronetic (that is, practical, situational, based in experience) rather than rational, as the Enlightenment understood rationality. So for him modern conservative thought became possible only when romanticism was combined with estate-thinking. And that connection was first made by a now rather obscure German political theorist named Adam Müller.

Müller is the primary focus of Schmitt's book, too. But Schmitt's understanding of postrevolutionary German thought is very different from Mannheim's. He insists that romanticism is *not* a conservatism but rather (to use a language that is not his own) a pivotal moment in the development of modern subjectivity at large. Schmitt pursues this argument less as a modern conservative à la Mannheim than as a Catholic ultraconservative in de Maistre's tradition. But he does so with a startling existentialist and polarizing twist. For Schmitt, at this stage of his career, politics is based on a *terrible decision*, the decision between good and evil (Schmitt 1986, 71). If a social program or act does not proceed from such a decision, then, for Schmitt, it is not political at all. We can recognize here an intimation of the later Schmitt, for whom politics is independent of morality, being instead based in a fiercely polarized order divided between friends and enemies.

To pursue his argument, Schmitt sketches out an extraordinary genealogy for romanticism. He argues that the key structures of modern intellectual and political life appear in none other than the seventeenth-century French Catholic (Oratorian) philosopher and priest Nicolas Malebranche, who attempted further to reconcile Cartesianism to Christian orthodoxy.[6] The analysis runs like this: the Cartesian method had created a new philosophical problem with powerful implications for all rational thought. It had made it difficult to clarify how immaterial entities (the soul, the will, reason) acted upon the physical world and, in particular, since causal chains were confined to material objects, how human intentions could function as agents. As Schmitt sees it, Malebranche's solution was to replace a concept of the "occasion" for that of "cause" in the everyday world. In the skeptical tradition, Malebranche accepted that the immanent world was not ordered by rationality. God became "the only true cause of every single psychic and physical event. God brings about the inexplicable correspondence of mental and corporeal phenomena. Everything taken together . . . is a mere occasion for God's activity. In fact, it is not the human being who acts, but rather God" (86). In other words, for Malebranche, God is a sovereign power and actant in every single event whatever, and without God, a meaningless, denuded universe, like that later supposed by the radically skeptical David Hume, comes into being. (Schmitt does not tell us that both Francis Hutcheson and David Hume developed their groundbreaking secular philosophies by accepting Malebranche's skeptical analyses of immanent morality and causality and declining to rescue them by God's omniscient activity and capacity to create ex nihilo, leaving immanent experience—Hume—or immanent moral nature—Hutcheson—to do God's work.)[7]

Schmitt's argument about Malebranche's contribution to the history of modernity is bold and simple. Malebranche himself had sanctioned a "legitimist passivity" proper to seventeenth-century absolutism (98), and he did indeed (as Schmitt was probably not aware) become a cult figure among English nonjurors (Anglicans who declined to declare loyalty to William and Mary and their Hanoverian successors on divine-right grounds) precisely for this reason. Nonetheless, Malebranche's occasionalism structures modern thought since modernity has replaced God—or, more exactly, his omnipresent ceaselessly creative God—with other endlessly creative sovereign powers. First of all, modern enlightened and revolutionary thought replaces God with society so that, from the left's point of view, what happens in the human world is always understood as caused socially. Individuals are puppets of social forces, and liberal progressivism's political aim is to realize social structures able fully to extend and energize individual capacities and experiences that its theoretical presuppositions degrade. In riposte, modern counterrevolutionary conservatism replaces God with history: for conservatism, history underpins and secures the human order, individuals being its playthings (82). And, last, the romantics replace God with the self—for them life becomes a series of occasions for the individual's own self-expansion, imaginative flights, or heightenings of the world.

This account of modernity is starkly at odds with the more received liberal one that thinks of modernization as the gradual empowerment of individuals, since, as just noted, for Schmitt neither progressivism, nor conservatism, nor romanticism actually ground agency in free individuals. The logic of this is clear in the cases of progressivism and conservatism, since in them society and history are respectively deemed the primary engines of human activity. But what about romanticism, which, after all, Schmitt considers to have invented sovereign subjectivity? The point is that, because the romantics treat the world as a series of occasions, a series of solicitations to intensity, to enchantment, to imaginative flight, to experience, they are actually in thrall to time and the world's flow. This is Schmitt's negative version of Mannheim's argument that romantics desire experience for its own sake. By the same stroke, romanticism retreats from actively shaping the world. But that retreat is enacted through romantic irony, by means of which romantics can simultaneously engage and disengage from the world (if in very different terms than that of Pauline bicameral spirituality, for instance) and which, as it were, allows them to feel and know themselves as propelled into endless provisionality.

Schmitt's main argument, then, is that the basis of political agency—the capacity to take the terrible decision—is severely compromised in romanticism, where what replaces commitment to good or to evil is serialized assent and affect, mood, interest.

> The problem of occasionalism is not merely metaphysical; it is just as much an ethical problem. It concerns the ancient question of human free will: the question of the status and content of human activity. Of course the . . . romantic . . . did, *eo ipso*, everything. He was responsible only to his autonomous ego. But in practice, everything and nothing are really identities in such cases, and the question remains: What does human activity consist in?

> According to the ethic of the systems of occasionalism, it is only in emotion. A moral (*sittlicher*) act is an act of evaluation. The person accompanies the act of another person with his assent [*Zustimmung*] or rejection, with an affirmative or negative judgment. His freedom consists in "assent," [*consentement*: Schmitt uses the French word here] in a feeling of value, a judgment, and a criticism. It is precisely the ethics of rationalistic systems that for limiting the person to "assenting" ["consensus": Schmitt uses the English word here] to the immutable nomological necessity [*Gesetzmässigkeit*] of the event. In romanticism, however, this idea also is sentimentalized and deformed in an emotive direction. This also begins as early as Malebranche. God creates and produces. The human being follows the event with his feelings. In this way, however, he participates in the process. Where true reality was clearly and unambiguously perceived, as in Malebranche . . . the impression of being an *occasio* in the hand of God did not exclude a consciousness of responsibility. Human beings, who are firmly rooted in their religious, social, and national milieu, belong to the community that grows around them and with which they themselves grow. It is different when occasionalism is subjectified: in other words, when the isolated subject treats the world as an *occasio*. In that case the activity of the subject consists only in the fanciful animation of its affect. . . . His activity is the affective echo of an activity that is necessarily not his own. (94)

Here we find further traces of Mannheim's thesis, but pushed toward Catholicized Burkeanism. Romantic subjectivity is a product of the collapse of the old corporatist order and the rejection of Catholicism. But, for Schmitt, because the romantic is no longer connected to a particular "religious, social, and national milieu" and bends to whatever social forces structure experience, she cannot be a conservative either. No conservative can assent to post-Malebranchean political modernity. And Schmitt points to Müller's career of inconstancy—he moved from affirming revolutionary principles to defending legitimism in the service of Metternich—as a key example of a "political romanticism" that can embrace conservatism as readily as it can embrace emancipatory revolution. For Schmitt, it was only at the end of Müller's life, when he returned to Catholicism in true piety, that anything like a possibility of true, engaged, conservative politics in the full sense became available to him (49–50).

So where does this brief account of two early-twentieth-century theories of conservatism leave us in relation to critique today?

Clearly, the Mannheim–Schmitt exchange does not do justice to modern conservatism's intellectual complexity and variety. Nor does it adequately reflect the intellectual path that Mannheim or Schmitt were each to take over the decades to come. But what it does show is one way in which critique's purposes can be thought of and acted upon without appeal to universal reason, without revolutionary hope, and especially without hope for more and better democracy. And, in the process, this exchange also clarifies the constitutive divisions of modernity's political terrain. Both theorists agree that once the Enlightenment's project acquires political force after 1789, then social thought and experience becomes politicized in the sense that they cannot avoid being placed not necessarily *in* but at least *in relation to* the contest between progress and reaction. So, potentially at least, there exist three zones—progressive thought, conservative thought, and neutral thought. Neutral thought needs to be distinguished from the classical "contemplative life," for instance, because it describes less a chosen, individual path distant from, but in harmony with, "active life" than a withdrawal into values, sensibilities, and methods of thought that are not able to be accommodated to the political scene and that are, for that very reason, politically significant. (Indeed, Schmitt will later argue that democratic liberalism becomes that mode of thought which wants to implement systemic consensual neutrality as the authoritative mode of governmentality.) As far as we are concerned here, the key difference between the two thinkers is that Mannheim argues that retreat from the political is itself a conservative move, while Schmitt contends that, since politics is constituted in decision and action, neutrality is possible but that neutrality (namely romanticism) in democratic polities actually involves effective serial assent to whatever party dominates at a particular moment, whether conservative or progressive.

It follows that the questions to ask of the contemporary humanities concern not just their historical relation to conservatism and progressivism but to their neutrality and inscription into the affective practices of political assent. This way of stating the matter may seem to downgrade the left's historical prominence within the humanities. But I would argue that that history is for the most part recent, being largely confined to the period of emancipation struggles in the 1960s, when previously disenfranchised groups fought not just for social equality but to retrieve their histories and cultures. The humanities were an important vehicle for those retrievals.

But, on the one hand, those emancipation movements have now been integrated into global democratic state capitalism and carry less and less continuing radical political charge, and, on the other, the humanities wing of the 1960s "identity" and postcolonial emancipation movements were, to a considerable extent, conservative themselves. In the main, they aimed to add the weight of heritage and identity to the struggle for social and political access and recognition.

In general, then, and as both Mannheim and Schmitt imply, the humanities belong mainly either to conservatism or to neutrality. And, as we shall further see in the next chapter, the disciplines we are most concerned with—English and cultural studies—are in fact solidly grounded in conservatism.

T. S. Eliot was the key figure in the emergence of both. In particular, in the period around World War I, under the influence of T. E. Hulme and Action Française, he developed the techniques of modern literary criticism in order to counter modernity's perceived depredations on experience itself, a program that belongs exactly to Mannheim's moment. In regard to cultural studies: around the period of World War II and of the prophetic fear of "totalitarian democracy," Eliot turned to the concept "culture" precisely against Mannheim's embrace of "planning for freedom." In a theophanized Burkean mode and supplementing the Maurrassian notion of "civilization" by the ethnographical concept of culture, he named culture "a whole way of life." "Whole" because it covered all social groups but also, more to the point, because it covered all life experiences and possibilities too and, hence, for Eliot must ultimately be grounded in religion. For him, no secular way of life could be whole. And culture thought religiously could legitimate resistance to the social democratic state apparatus and its deployments of expert scientific knowledge. British cultural studies as we know it is born once Richard Hoggart and Raymond Williams appropriate Eliot's conservative, Anglican concept of culture—and its political program—for secular laborist socialism and the democratic state education system.[8]

Clearly, contemporary literary and cultural studies are no longer organized by anything like the conservatism in which they originated: they have neutralized themselves. It is at this point that the question of the contemporary polity and Schmitt's narrow notion of the political reenters, however. For I'd argue that contemporary democratic state capitalism has reached a stage where neutrality is in fact not a fit option for the academic humanities, such is the extent to which the humanities have been intruded upon and commanded by compulsory/fundamental democracy and its dedemocratizing processes. Especially in nations where the state funds and thence controls higher education, endgame capitalism demands that the humanities too serve (the state's understanding of) the market and the nation and in so doing refuses them real autonomy. But the humanities, and not least literary and cultural studies, cannot accede to those demands without jeopardizing the practices and values that shape and sanction them. These practices and values do still (in part) belong to the nonoccasionalist "solidarity" with the world and the resistant "germ of experience" that adheres to memories of this solidarity, albeit within a limited, institutionalized pedagogical setting. They also, as it were, take the place of the truncated lineage of critique, whose political and philosophical underpinnings (the binding of reason to the will for radical change) have been eroded, as we have seen. We must now defend our care for language and signifying systems from elsewhere in time and space; our commitment to expression and imagination as ends in themselves; and our practices of deliberation, attention, speculation, and debate in the search for truth.

No less importantly (if less ambitiously), we are to defend the *institutions* of the academic humanities as organized sites where groups of people gather collectively to examine, discuss, conserve, and transmit the past as it exists in texts, archives, images, and so on and to maintain standards through their power of accreditation. Which is to say, to engage in academic life by and large protected from the instrumental purposes and structures of institutions that are more tightly integrated into democratic state capitalism. To think like this—that the humanities are important as institutions apart from their role as bearers of value—is to return to a certain Burkean conservatism, since Burke (and Müller) insisted on the primary importance of particular institutions and constitutions to social order and meaning. But, under this aspect, it is a Burkean conservatism whose ethical and cultural content has been evacuated. From this perspective, the humanities are valuable because they happen in organizations bound to particular rules and to particular well-established protocols of conduct (or "personae") that inquisitively attend to certain kinds of objects and not because, for instance, they support critique, or the pursuit of civilized life or rich experiences, or even the search for truth.

This *institutional* defense of the humanities is posed very directly against our "managers" and "leaders" as these come into being in universities committed to democratic state capitalist reformism but that are themselves much less democratic still than the traditionally constituted humanities. All the more so since the various post-1960s political programs that the academic humanities directed toward the larger world—the demand for justice, for recognition of oppressed identities, hopes for unimaginable revolutions to come, the description of ongoing social destitution, the demand for better and more democracy, and so on—in the end have just solidified the market-state's instrumentalization of the education sector.

Let me be clear about this argument's political implications. I don't believe that the resistance that I am now invoking from out of conservatism can be organized as a movement or that it can, in its own interest, join either formal party politics or radical movement politics. Or that it will be widely embraced even inside the humanities. Or, as I say, that it can either stimulate or lean on articulated and active refusals of democratic state capitalism itself. The resistance that the humanities are compelled toward is not just unorganized but less than clearly visible or fully acknowledged: it's a structural and thence, in a sense, an ideal resistance. And it is, to some degree, esoteric in the Straussian mode: in practice, it cannot declare itself on all occasions, even in all classrooms, without defeating itself. But it is fit and true for all that. At any rate, it's as if Schmitt's and Mannheim's old tripartite order—divided between progressivism, conservatism, and neutrality—has collapsed, leaving the humanities in a condition of recalcitrant obedience, a straitjacketed enmity toward the state-market combination and its academic-bureaucratic machinery, an enmity neither quite neutral nor engaged and in part protected by sheer organizational inertia, but which for all that does turn us, in our search for succor and a basis for (or replacement of) critique, toward lineages of conservative refusal of the postrevolutionary order.

FOUR

Literary Criticism's Failure

As I have suggested, up until World War II serious literature was inhospitable to democratization's purposes and processes, at least in Europe. So too, as many scholars have noted, was literary criticism (see Asher 1995, Weimann 1974, Williams 1958). In the light of the previous chapters, this bald statement immediately solicits a number of further questions. Where does literary criticism fit into the account of reform, refusal, conservatism, and critique that I have been sketching? Is literary criticism's nondemocratic heritage one reason for its apparent loss of influence and confidence over the last few decades? Has criticism, at least in its original counter-democratic form, indeed failed? If so, what does that mean for literary studies and the humanities more generally?

One useful way to begin to address questions like these is to examine the forces and energies that first shaped criticism. This may even help to establish what its current strengths and purposes are—after all, a return to origins is a familiar strategy for renovation within spiritual and intellectual institutions. Latin Christianity, for instance, has often attempted a revitalizing return to "primitive Christianity." In difficult times, philosophy too has returned for inspiration to its putative Greek sources. For literary studies, however, this move is more problematic not just because the discipline is not dogmatic, not just because our founders lack the first Greek philosophers' heroic status, but precisely because anyone embarking upon it will quickly realize that they are headed toward recovering another modern conservatism. And it remains institutionally and intellectually risky to negotiate a positive relation to conservatism, even along the lines suggested in the previous chapter.

Modern literary criticism, as practiced in the academy, is sui generis. It's surprisingly removed from Aristotle's or Boileau's classical criticism, for instance, or even from Samuel Coleridge's or Friedrich Schlegel's romantic criticism. What constitutes and underpins this difference? The answer becomes clearer if we turn to a moment immediately prior to its invention, when British literary intellectuals began agitating for the university study of English and, in the same breath, for a new relation between the discipline and the state.

The most important such intervention was made by John Churton Collins, a well-known journalist, textbook editor, and university-extension lecturer, who had taught across Britain and the United States. Involved in the efforts to establish a chair of English literature at Oxford in the 1880s, he became English studies' most formidable champion. In his *The Study of English Literature: A Plea for Its Recognition and Organization at the Universities* (1891), which won support from a wide range of public figures, Collins complains that, although the state had accepted responsibility for both technical education and primary and secondary schooling, it had not yet supported liberal-arts pedagogy.[1]

According to Collins, the disciplined study of English was necessary because the system now needed to shape citizens' characters so they could take full advantage and control of democratic enfranchisement. That is, drawing on policies associated with the philosophical radicals of the 1830s, Collins was responding to the incipient emergence of the social democratic state, which, despite serious contestation, was then taking on limited responsibility for the cultivation of the nation's citizens as well as for their welfare and security. Surprisingly, he believed that classical Athens and Rome provided a model of centralized social democratic education, since in classical antiquity education was regarded as a tool of cultivation in the senses that he required, namely (to use his own phrasing) ethically, politically, morally, and aesthetically (Collins 1891, 4). Today, ethically, so Collins argued, the "interpretation of Literature" could "effect for popular culture what it is of power to effect," that is, as he cites the Liberal politician John Morley saying, it could protect against "the disgorgements of the cheap popular press—with its superficial second-hand criticism, its flimsy summaries of the results of original scholarship or research, its slovenly vulgar editions of the English classics, and its irrepressible floods of sloppy, foolish, illiterate fiction" (112). Politically, literary study could warn, admonish, and guide (4). And as a means of "moral and aesthetic education," it could "exercise . . . influence on taste, on tone, on sentiment, on opinion, on character" (4). All this under the guidance of a center—the state.

So literary study is necessary to shape and contain democracy. But Collins's curriculum lacks anything that we can recognize as criticism as such. In particular, it contained nothing like what we have to come call "close reading," the practice of which, of course, lies at the heart of the English department to this day and which was to confer upon criticism its full legitimacy and prestige. Criticism in its modern guise became the focus of English studies only after World War I, and it did so, I'd suggest, at a specific place—the University of Cambridge, in the work of T. S. Eliot, I. A. Richards, and F. R. Leavis.

It did so when these critics appealed to three concepts in particular. The most important of these was none other than *experience*. Indeed, literary criticism emerged as a specific academic discipline, independent of literary history, philology, and rhetoric, first by figuring literature as (in Leavis's words) the "poetic-creative use of language—the use by which the stuff of experience is presented to speak and act for itself" (Leavis 1978, 110), and then by defining itself as "the endeavour to discriminate between experiences and to evaluate them," to cite Richards's 1924 *Principles of Literary Criticism* (Richards 1928, 2). With the horror of the war unforgotten, and as a contribution to what has come to be called "modernism," English studies could sharpen its opposition to the destabilizing and debasing cultural consequences of industrialization, militarism, modernization, and democracy by appealing not to conventional and bankrupt categories like civilization, wisdom, and gentlemanly cultivation, but to what I have been thinking of as the elemental particle of being-in-the-world under democracy: the experience itself, thought of as the basic unit of what Henry James named "felt life." So, paradoxically, criticism could assert close reading's full importance only by centering literary analysis on experience rather than on linguistic, aesthetic, or rhetorical categories. Indeed, literary criticism's appeal to experience is designed to refuse the limits and vocabularies of the aesthetic in particular. And critics came to call the faculty that could be trained to respond to experience—that is, to respond to complex experiences and to discriminate between experiences—not the aesthete's "taste" but rather "sensibility," wresting that term from sentimentalism as it did so.

The second key concept for modern literary criticism was "impersonality," through which a form of classicism apparent in Collins (and, of course, elsewhere) could decisively rebut both what was considered as romantic subjectivism and the contemporary "new humanism," which, from the critics' perspective, was providing ethical cover for modernization's wrecking force, including the passions that led to war.

More problematically, literary criticism's last constitutive concept was history or, rather, a particular notion of history that assumed, first, that changing social structures were imprinted in experiences themselves and, then, that relations between literature and society have been degraded over the democratizing period in ways that required criticism to present itself as a tool for cultural resistance and renewal.

T. S. Eliot

Let's start this brief conspectus with T. S. Eliot. His inaugurating contribution to the new discipline, mainly written in 1919, did not involve any effort toward its academic institutionalization. The new mode of criticism first appeared in Eliot's journalism for the literary weekly *The Athenaeum*, and it did so no doubt indirectly as a response to the war's delegitimization of prevailing social and cultural standards, progressive or not.[2] (Eliot and Richards did not fight in the war, but Leavis did, where he suffered from a serious trauma.) By 1919, however, Eliot had also completed his Harvard dissertation, *Knowledge and Experience in the Philosophy of F. H. Bradley*, in which he contributes to that reconfiguring of the concept of experience that had been a major philosophical enterprise since the 1880s. But, as we know, at this time he was also immersed in that mode of historicist, classicist, Maurrassian French literary theory that, for its own political purposes, aligned particular writers to particular cultural movements and, in general, sided with nonhumanist classicism.

Circa 1900, the philosophical understanding of experience had two features that are particularly pertinent to understanding the concept's absorption by literary criticism. First, for Eliot as well as for Bradley and William James, experience is considered as prior to the division between subject and object: "if, in seeking for reality, we go to experience, what we certainly do not find is a subject or an object," as Bradley put it (Bradley 1962, 146). And for Bradley in particular experience brings us closest to the "Absolute," to the real, which is not directly available to knowledge and truth. Instead, for Bradley and Eliot, experience forms an autonomous whole order, which ceaselessly divides into local clusters or centers, one of which is the self itself. (This marks these thinkers off from William James's radical empiricism, for instance, which contains no room for even that kind of self.) This line of thought—which aligns experience to impersonality, since selfhood is ontologically secondary and provisional and can be ascribed to formations larger than the individual (a caste, a state)—offers a way out of methodological individualism and metaphysical atomism. It has political consequences too, since its deindividuating force unsettles political liberalism, which arbitrarily grants priority to individual experiences and wills. So this account of experience, when applied to literature, can at least potentially make literature increasingly available both to collectivism and to conservatism. On a different front, that constitutive impersonality is why experience will also appeal to Bataille and Blanchot, although in them, as we have seen, "experience" mutates into an antihumanist spiritual performance bound to the act of writing itself.

The second key feature of experience as theorized in the period was Wilhelm Dilthey's distinction between *Erlebnis* and *Erfahrung*, which for our purposes can be thought of as the distinction between *the experience* as it happens serially in a moment and *experience* as accumulated knowledge and practical skill, that is, experience as thought, action, and participation's "child"—to use Benjamin Disraeli's figure for what he calls experience's "genealogy" (Disraeli 1853, 176–177).

For Eliot in his dissertation as for Bradley, all our relations to the world occur as experiences, so that all that is knowable is experience.[3] Within our experiences, however, particular knowable objects appear as "points of attention." Objects always and only result from an effort of attention (Eliot 1964, 157). As to truth: truth makes claims on the real, not on objects qua objects. However, since the real is not knowable in itself, truth is always a matter of interpretation, with the corollary that there is no difference except in degree between interpretation and description (164). Furthermore, no interpretation is normatively neutral: interpretation is understood as "a valuation and an assignment of meaning" (165). For Eliot, it is also the case that the only "significant experiences" occur outside convention and *doxa*'s web. But such experiences also tend toward the arbitrary and, indeed, the mad. Here the figure of the critic enters: significant experiences are protected from disorder by "the true critic," who is "a scrupulous avoider of formulae" and who "refrains from states that pretend to be literally true," knowing that her "truths are the truths of experience rather than of calculation" (164).

Neither Eliot nor Bradley consider the relationship between language and experience in great detail, but it should already be clear that Eliot assumes that experiences are semantic in that they always possess meaning: he accepts that "no experience escapes the despotism of significance" as Michael Oakeshott, also from within Bradleyean idealism, later pithily phrased it (Oakeshott 1933, 25–26). That is why experiences need to be protected from repetition, emotionalism, and uniformity. So even if Eliot was not interested in establishing connections between his academic philosophy, his literary journalism, his politics, and his poetry (and he often was), it follows from his philosophical work that (1) the critic's task is to objectify experiences by closely attending to the literary work. The more concrete the quality of attention to words on the page, the greater the objectivity and particularity of the literary experience. And (2) criticism's task will be to assess experiences in terms of a significance to be measured, in the first instance, by their remoteness from the commonplace and the general as well as from private arbitrariness.

Eliot's early criticism extends and breaks from his commentary on Bradley by distinguishing the work of emotion from that of intelligence and contemplation, since now it is emotion, whether the reader's or the writer's, that is associated with the "accidents of personal association" (Eliot 1928, 6) extrinsic to the literary work itself. In something of a conceptual leap, this means that intelligent appreciation of literature engages with content only secondarily. Such appreciation primarily attends to medium and "structure," both in the individual work and in the atemporal order of literature as a whole. We can put it like this: for Eliot, literary form is to content roughly as experience is to its (unknowable) object. The first provides the structuring conditions for cognizing the second. Further, critical attention to form starves the merely personal response: it staves off subjectivity. It is this heightening of form's functionality, along with the insistence that form is experience's vehicle, that enables Eliot to think that successful literature involves an "extinction of personality" on the reader's and the writer's behalf. Nonetheless, good literature uses its medium both so that "impressions and experiences combine in peculiar and unexpected ways" (56) and so that "sensory experiences" are sufficiently objectified to invoke a particular emotion (100). For criticism tuned to consider literature like this, and if in some tension with the idealist's tendency to merge interpretation and description, the literary text is fundamentally uninterpretable—"qua work of art the work of art cannot be interpreted" (96)—in the same way that one experience cannot be translated into another experience. It is because literature is primarily experiential that texts are uninterpretable, just as it is because literature is experience that its forms may become fragmented into discrete evocative moments. Furthermore, in relation to literature a critic's interpretation may quickly become an expression of a merely personal insight or, worse, an exercise in the display of personal ingenuity. Yet—and this is crucially important—critics, who cannot settle for mere description, cannot establish general rules or principles as criteria for judgment in their acts of discrimination either. To escape the abiding seductiveness of abstraction and routinization or of subjectivity, critics are restricted to comparing one literary text to another, singly, outside of any rules or formulae, more or less mutely.

At this point, Eliot turns to history. In the period around 1920, he argued that in England the capacity to experience deteriorated soon after John Donne's death, when the "intellect ceased to be at the tip of the senses," when the language became less and less capable of providing "words perpetually juxtaposed in new and sudden combinations," and when it ceased to be the case that "sensation became word, and the word . . . sensation" (117).[4] Eliot here is articulating a version of Maulnier's later argument concerning classicism's gradual reduction into mere "intelligence" and doing so by aligning what Eliot was to call "the supersession of ontology by psychology" to those forces of republicanism, liberalism, and democratization, of which, for him, Milton stands as an early champion and of which the year 1640 (when Parliament rebelled against Charles I's absolutist monarchy) stands as a signal marker (Eliot 1994, 90). Or, to state Eliot's argument slightly differently, after the "puritan" revolution, literary language became more disjoined from the object (that is, from the attended/evoked experience; Eliot 1928, 149), and it did so as individual consciousnesses became detached both from the objective world and from unified Christian Europe. Indeed, by Algernon Swinburne's time, "language uprooted [had] adapted itself to an independent life of atmospheric nourishment" (149). This means that literary critics are involved in a struggle "against the continual deterioration of language" in relation to experience (8). They are involved in maintaining a resistant tradition or, as Eliot's followers will more often say, in maintaining resistant *continuities*. The critic's weapon in this struggle is an organized attention to (1) literary structure, (2) literary tradition, and (3) the new writing, in which that tradition may be extended and transformed. In effect, Eliot is urging a dehistoricized historicism: a double temporality in which modern history—under the impulsion of Protestantism, romanticism, and democracy—progressively disjoins language from experience, while literary tradition changes shape each time it welcomes a new work (and in particular, around 1919, works that mimic disorder to invoke order) so as to protect language's adequacy to experience from history's predations.

I. A. Richards

Eliot's literary critical program first took academic shape with I. A. Richards.[5] This is surprising because Richards's intellectual and political orientation was very different from Eliot's. He had been a student of the anti-idealist G. E. Moore and had interests in academic psychology (especially Gestalt theory, psychoanalysis, and Pavlovian behaviorism) as well as the new language-centered "analytic" philosophy that Moore helped develop after 1920.[6] Richards began teaching English literature at Cambridge in 1919, and in 1926, when the subject was given a new curriculum and placed in the

Faculty of Archaeology and Anthropology so as to detach it from philology, he was hired as a university lecturer. That appointment acknowledged that his *Principles of Literary Criticism* (1924) had legitimated the new field by removing it from both belle-lettrism and philology.

Richards grounded literary studies as a discipline both intellectually and practically by reformulating Eliot's conservative project for a modernized version of Collins's institutional activism on the basis of the latest scientific psychology and on what Leavis was later to call his characteristic "neo-Benthamism" (Leavis 1978, 135). In *Principles of Literary Criticism*, Richards is concerned first to demonstrate the social value of the aesthetic in general: "What is the value of the arts?" he begins by asking (Richards 1928, 4), and he answers that the aesthetic realm provides uniquely complex, unified, and harmoniously structured experiences to autonomous subjects. Literature, in particular, can develop the senses when it animates the full semantic range of, and connections between, words and phrases as well as when it uses tropes that surprise us into "realizations" (to use one of his terms of art), that is, into experiences of which we are conscious yet that, in their concreteness, have the force of the real. For Richards (as for Eliot), writers can use language to realize experience when they possess faculties that can respond to, remember, and combine a rich range of different experiences to start with. There is a smooth movement from life to writing via the creative artist's psychological constitution (see Needham 1982, 26). And literary experience has a precise psychological function: it reconciles opposing impulses, thence giving pleasure. Finally, the literary experience heightens and extends experiences and capabilities more generally. When we read good literature, "We seem to feel that our command of life, our insight into it and our discrimination of its possibilities, is enhanced, even for situations having little or nothing to do with the subject of the reading" (Richards 1928, 185). Thence literature and literary criticism's unique importance to democratic education.

The appeal to experience—against truth and belief—is crucial, since once again the transitivity of literary and lived experiences also allows literature to salve social damage. Aesthetic experiences are also ethically essential for historical reasons. Richards, like Arnold and Collins before him, contends that literary experience can resist the "commercialism" that threatens a "transvaluation by which popular taste replaces trained discrimination" (36). But he argues further that "customs change more slowly than conditions" (56), and, this being so, art is where new conditions first produce coherent but complex experiences proper both to human potential and to the times, namely experiences that neither tear affect from thought nor are bound to reactionary "occultism, absolutes and arbitrariness" (58) nor to the limiting discourse of virtue and vice (61). In *Science and Poetry* (1926), the literary experience forms the endpoint of a radically immanent and antireligious worldview in which "experience is its own justification" (79) and that alone can stimulate what is truly valuable, "the fullest, keenest, most active and completest kind of life" (41). Democratizing statements like these bring Richards close to that pragmatism à la William James, which Eliot had been in flight from since his Harvard days. It is exactly the limits that Richards places on the uses of literary criticism for moral and social "salvation" that Eliot demurred from in his review of the book (Eliot 1927, 243; cf. Leavis 1978, 134–135).

Richards also departs from Eliot by the force with which he insists that literary texts *communicate*. It is this that requires their formalization, their use of symbols (that is, of experiences that elicit other experiences), and their stripping away of "personal particularities" (Richards 1926, 78). For him, to repeat, literary experience is uniquely valuable in that it enables a Schillerian harmonization of faculties—it can reconcile divergent or opposing senses of a poem, say. And it is because literature presents experience within an organized verbal communication which "keeps it from being a mere welter of disconnected impulses" (36). Nonetheless, the transmission of experience trumps the transmission of interpretable meaning: poets and their readers are to be interested in not what "a poem says . . . but what it is" (34–35), just because the poem communicates not a message or a truth but a significant experience. It's in these terms that, for Richards, literary works can become "simply the best data available for deciding what experiences are more valuable than others" (32). And, in a further (leftish) move, he claims that literary texts may provide the ground for wider social cooperation (136), just because they offer stable and impersonal experiences by virtue of their communicability.

As to criticism: while teaching at Cambridge, Richards launched an ethnographical project on students and colleagues, recording their responses to anonymous poems of varying quality (Richards 1929, 4). What he found was that students, who had succumbed to the mediascape of the time, typically failed to understand not so much what the poems *said* as what they *expressed*. Students did not grasp "the experience, the *mental conditions* relevant to the poems" (10). As a result, Richards realized that criticism must focus on a poem's "minute particulars," for only then could its experiential ambivalence, suggestiveness, nuances, and complex admixtures of thought and emotion be uncovered. Here again, it's a poem's psychological rather than linguistic complexity that neither any casual attention nor any constative proposition can catch. And Richards carefully itemizes the various kinds of response that prevent readers from distinguishing between significant experiences and routinized ones. Such bad reading habits include "mnenomic irrelevances," "stock responses," "sentimentality," "inhibitions," and "doctrinal adhesions." Richards also notes two crippling *professional* presuppositions—first, those that he calls "technical," that is, the false assumption that it is the poem's use of language rather than its effect upon us that is the proper object of critical attention, whose consequence will be "dogmatic pronouncements upon detail" (277), and, then, "critical presuppositions," that is, any theory about, or any application of rules for, what a poem should be or do (283). In the end, just as a poem requires careful attention because it is an expression of an experience rather than a mere linguistic artifact, criticism must not lapse into interpretation, since it needs to judge whether "new experience can or cannot be taken into the fabric [of past experiences and developed habits of mind] with advantage" (285).

F. R. Leavis

Although F. R. Leavis modified his position in important ways across the course of his career, all his writings remain recognizably within the paradigm established by his immediate predecessors Eliot and Richards, although his politics (which moved rightward over his career) were, in the end, closer to the first than the second.[7] Indeed, it is with Leavis and his followers that modern academic criticism revealed its full potentiality as well as its limits. That's because, especially after about 1940, when his aim to stimulate a knowledgeable and critical reading public through his journal *Scrutiny* floundered, Leavis was committed to harnessing the full power of the democratic state's education system on literary criticism's behalf.[8] By that time, Eliot and Richards were elsewhere engaged: Eliot, in full retreat from capitalist modernity, had turned to High Anglicanism, and Richards, as part of Harvard's Education Faculty, was working to extend communicative rationality and critical literacy. But Leavis was building an institution he called the English School and was insisting that democratic capitalism could not simply be refused or retreated from and that literature that did retreat from society (like most Victorian poetry, he thought) was unworthy of serious critical attention. He and his followers established journals, built bridges between the tertiary and secondary education sectors, fixed a canon (in which the requirements of the curriculum magically harmonized with the heritage's number of masterworks), and fostered academic disciples. Most of all, they insisted on literary criticism's social seriousness: nothing mattered more than a critically endorsed canon in efforts to build a good democratic and capitalist society.

At Leavisism's core lay a classroom moment in which the critic-teacher guided students to value the best writing approximately as Eliot and Richards understood it. In a seminar discussion, the teacher asked students to compare passages from different texts by attending to the concreteness of each—especially in their tropes—as well as to how tightly form cohered to content, a collective act of attention in which any signifier might be revealed as unexpectedly important. This careful comparative scrutiny, attuned to fine surprises, culminated not simply in the teacher offering a judgment of one particular text's greater capacity to objectify a full and significant experience but in pointing to words on the page and then asking the students to accept a literary judgment: "That's so, isn't it?" Or, as Leavis framed this comparative pedagogical question in "Criticism and Philosophy," "This kind of thing—don't you find it so?—wears better than that" (Leavis 1978, 215).

The authoritative solicitation of student assent was only contingently attached to interpretation, since for Leavis, as for Eliot and Richards, interpretation as such would smother and personalize the discrimination of experiences. It is worth noting that, in the Leavisite classroom, authoritative solicitation of an assent to judgment after analysis repeats the freedom/necessity relation within Kantian aesthetics, since the teacher-critic requires the student's *assent* to a judgment in order for the student's literary experience to be free (and so their own), while the teacher's insistence on a particular judgment is required if that freedom is not to fall prey to arbitrariness and subjectivism.

Yet the first literary-critical category to feel the stress under Leavisism is experience. For Leavis, literature, at its best, was able to evoke less "the ordinary experience of life in time" and more the experiences of "supremely illuminating significance," as he put it in response to Eliot's *Four Quartets* (Leavis 1943, 92). So the literary canon becomes not just a register of impersonal, revelatory, unified encounters with the world but a suggestion or symbol of unworlded possibilities, orientation toward which, however, is a moral accomplishment, an expression of an especially finely trained sensibility. The literary experience becomes less a balanced *Erlebnis* and more an elevated *Erfahrung* sometimes directed toward that "kind of profound impersonality" associated with tragedy, sometimes, almost eschatologically, directed toward an unrealized future (Leavis 1978, 130). In Leavis's later work, the aspirational character of the literary experience is conceived of as a humanly fundamental and vital creativity—the "living principle"—which, it goes almost without saying, drives both great writers and great critics and which supplements actual fallen social conditions and does so by refusing the temptations of both liberal individualism and utilitarianism.

Leavis's replacement of *Erlebnis* by *Erfahrung* is partly driven by his having a more developed sociological understanding than Eliot and Richards. For him, the connection between social structures and experience is so strong that the experiential flow from reading to living, and thus literature's utility, to which Richards in particular was committed, cannot easily be affirmed. After all, individuals are formed *socially* rather than ethically through their reading. It is clear that Leavis's years of teaching, his sensitivity to the hierarchical nature of the education system, along with his solid connections to secondary-school English meant that he fully understood the difficulties not just of effectively teaching criticism but of the barriers in using literature to realize and perfect experience in the larger world. For him, society stands between readers and texts—democratic capitalism in particular is not especially hospitable to literature—in part just because it prevents individuals from breaking out of their individuality.

The second category to feel the stress was history. When, in 1943, Leavis presented a detailed curriculum for an English School, commentators were surprised how much history, or rather historical sociology, it contained. Topics he presented for discussion included "Calvinism to Puritan individualism," "Church and State," "The reaction against Whig history," "The rise of Capitalism," "Economic individualism," "The causes of the civil war," "The revolution of 1688," "the social-economics correlations of literary history," and "the rise of the Press" (Leavis 1943, 52–53). In effect, he fleshed out and extended Eliot's Tory understanding of the past by connecting it to different, often more progressive, social histories, notably John and Barbara Hammond's left-liberal account of industrialization's destructive wake, R. H. Tawney's Christian Socialist critique of capitalism's impact upon community and charity, as well as some of Christopher Dawson's right-wing Catholic polemics against the Enlightenment. He was also influenced by contemporary works of sociology like Robert S. and Helen Merrell Lynd's *Middletown* (1937), which, according to Harold Laski, "drew an impressive contrast between democracy as an idea and democracy in action," and, most important, his wife Q. D. Leavis's *Fiction and the Reading Public* (1932), a historical critical analysis of the commercial market's destructive impact on literature (Laski 1949, 21). Leavisite literary criticism was, then, based on a countercapitalist or, as he later put it, a counter-"technological-Benthamite" historiography. For the younger Leavis especially, one could not be a literary critic except *against* liberal democratic capitalism, even as one worked within the system.

But he also recognized that there was no return to a Tawneyesque "organic society" or even to Augustan order under Queen Anne (to which he inclined, more than did Eliot, because it supposedly constituted a reading public that had not yet been divided into high and low). These relatively coherent historical moments could survive as truncated memories only in the university and the English School itself. So for him the universities are not just "the recognized symbols of cultural tradition" but cultural tradition and order's "directing force," "having an authority that should check and control the blind drive onward of material and mechanical development, with its human consequences" (Leavis 1943, 16). Yet the university—and especially the English School—could shelter only an elect group: "The potentialities of human experience in any age are realized only by a tiny minority" (Leavis 1962, 16). Especially in the aftermath of World War II and the incorporation of the wider university sector into social democratic state planning, Leavis's task was to extend this minority into the population through the education system as a whole, especially the secondary schools, without losing sight of the fact that the conditions for genuine criticism did not exist in society as such and would thus only be available to the elect.[9]

I cannot here spell out the various routes through which the project of Eliot, Richards, and Leavis lapsed. One reason was that, despite the importance to the movement of Eliot's own poetic breakthrough, it could not quite cope with literary modernism, especially in prose fiction. So it fell out of touch with the most adventurous and perceptive writing of its own time. The Leavisite emphasis on discriminating between experiences meant that it ended up being committed to literature where the gap between literature and life was least apparent. Thus Leavis dismissed the later, more experimental Henry James and his followers like Ivy Compton-Burnett and Elizabeth Bowen. He had no interest in writers like James Joyce and William Faulkner either, let alone in Kafka and Beckett. He even objected to E. M. Forster's breaks in verisimilitude. For him, it was as if the modernists had rejected the literary reformist project that, at least in the novel, he believed to be allied to realist mimesis. But more important to Leavisism's decline, of course, was the power of society's will to instrumentalism (especially to vocational education) along with its capacity to provide more immediate satisfactions than those offered by canonical literature. How could literary criticism of this kind compete with the energies through which students were led to accept those merely useful and pleasurable forms of subjectivity, rationality, and action that Leavisism was ultimately positioned against?

Leavisism never took hold in U.S. English departments. Admittedly, American New Criticism was founded as a conservative movement in Eliot's spirit by critics like Allen Tate and John Crowe Ransom, who attempted to harness the old Southern critique of Northern capitalist materialism to the new literary pedagogy. But New Criticism gradually accommodated itself to liberal capitalism and to the Cold War machinery of state as well as to the requirements of professional reproduction. It did so by displacing the social and ontological status of the literary text's unified ambiguity and complexity. Now canonical literature became not a reminder of more ordered and perfect social conditions (as for Eliot and Leavis) or a tool for psychological or moral individual development (as for Richards) but, on the one hand, the content of an autonomous cultural realm, that of the literary itself, whose highest metaphysical task was (as Ransom put it) to express "the way of the imagination in giving objective or Concrete existence to the homeless moral Universe," that is, to deploy literary language (language dense with ambiguity, figures, complexity, paradox) to articulate a world (usually conceived of as a modality of nature) that has been stripped of any transcendent purpose and relations and that has no literal, direct means of being communicated (Ransom 1955, 181). On the other hand, literature also bears witness to a pluralist world without absolutes, this argument being stated in its canonical form in Cleanth Brooks's *The Well Wrought Urn* (Brooks 1947, 256–257). In making these Spinozan and liberal democratic moves, and in order to fulfill its responsibility to literature's use of figure and indirection, New Criticism also elaborated the close-reading techniques first developed by Richards's student William Empson and quickly succumbed to the heresy of the brilliant interpretation, that is, to detaching interpretation from description, and to what Leavis denounced as the seconding of "the sense of value" to mere ingenuity (Leavis 1943, 71–72).[10] And as R. P. Blackmur pointed out with especial acuity, the New Critics' endless discovery and rediscovery, via close reading, of the properties of literary language in the texts that they most admired not only omitted a great deal of literature that did not use the language of ambiguity, complexity, and paradox at all but, more cripplingly still, failed to provide sufficient reason why this kind of literature was indeed uniquely important (see Weimann 1974, 96–97).

American critics who remained outside New Criticism also found it difficult to remain within the Cambridge school's project. Take Blackmur, who drew on Eliot's understanding of the relationship between literary language and experience and who, early in his career, was probably the major American critic closest to Leavisism and whom Leavis had in fact published in the 1930s. Yet Blackmur rarely engaged in close reading as experiential discrimination. Despite his sense that modernization has produced an intolerable society (he called himself a "conservative Christian anarchist" and a follower of Henry Adams, that strong antidemocrat) and despite his belief that literature best allows us to sense and know modernity's insufficiencies, Blackmur was more interested in sensitively defining a text's or oeuvre's particular literary mode (which is also a "mode of the psyche") than in pointing to literature's possibilities for life, as literary criticism originally demanded. The question of who reads literature and how was of little interest to him. Teaching at Princeton, he autonomized, sacralized, and pluralized literature in terms that leave capitalism and democratization to their own devices. And in the late 1940s, in *Eleven Essays on the European Novel*, he turned toward a vitalist religioethical criticism focused on good and evil as a means of recovering what he calls the "Christian-Greek picture" (Blackmur 1964, 46). Strangely, this led him to interpret even a political injustice like the anarchist Bartolomeo Vanzetti's execution in 1926 in Christological terms, positing Vanzetti's assumption of "the whole devastating guilt of the industrial society which killed him" (140).

Within Leavisism itself, which had no time for this kind of abstract religious turn, the pedagogy of authorized assent became routinized: Leavisite students dutifully and ceaselessly repeated the party line in a submissiveness that contradicted everything that literary criticism stood for. And Leavisism came undone along another track when the postwar left-Leavisites—in particular, Raymond Williams—found that Leavis's insistence on the rarity of literary criticism, its being the property of a "defensive minority," disregarded most people's "real social experience" and arrogantly dismissed the creativity and vitality of the cultural life of those who knew nothing of the literary canon (Williams 1958, 255; cf. Williams 1950, 29). The left-Leavisites accepted Leavis's (and Eliot's) critique of democratic capitalism, and (to a large degree) they joined the modern literary critical project itself, but they could not accede to what we would call that project's elitism. From this cultural-democratic point of view, great literature's experiential significance was being progressively diminished by literature's increasing remoteness from ordinary life in society. As a result, discrimination gradually became ideology critique, and, in this lineage, literary criticism mutated into cultural studies.

And, of course, after 1968, a poststructuralism, partly in the wake of Blanchot and Bataille, came to dominate literary theory, with an understanding of the relationship between history, language, and experience that opposed reformist pedagogic Leavisism at every level, since it was based on a displacement of social refusal onto the literary itself, as indicated above. The divorce of language from experience was now shaped as academic orthodoxy. Paradoxically, the linguistic turn helped hobble literary criticism: it broke its connection to wider social critique and to larger social purposes. And in a twinned move, implicit in the later New Criticism and clear in left-Leavisism, the universalism of the modernist category of experience was denounced. Whose experiences were Eliot, Richards, and Leavis talking about? Upon what social system does any "significant experience" rest? Whose particular privileges and interests lie cloaked in literary experience's claim to significance and universality?

And so, a century on, nothing positive remains of modern literary criticism in its original form, which is barely even a memory.

The obvious lesson to be learned from all this is that literary criticism cannot return to origins in any restorative spirit. Nonetheless, my feeling is that there are few alternatives to this barred return. English can no doubt continue as an academic discipline without any commitment to the literary criticism that first informed it, but only at the cost of its sense of purpose. This means that the field does need to reassert—or reconnoiter—the fundamental suppositions of literary criticism, in dialogue, admittedly, with the discipline's post-1968 transformations. And it needs, as much as it can, to avoid coerced assent. Again, those suppositions are (1) that literature preserves valuable (and nondemocratic) forms of experience; (2) that in literary texts, form is inseparable from content; (3) that an enlightened metaphysics of immanence is a condition for ascribing a supreme value to literary experience; (4) that literature, as criticism shapes it, exists both inside and outside of history; and (5) that the literary canon and its servants ultimately *oppose* democratic state capitalism and the commercial media, even if necessarily from within. We cannot, as I say, be confident that a criticism based on such propositions can now be articulated. If it were, it would likely be most energized by the last item on that list, by its (left-conservative) critique of and resistance to democratic capitalism's cultural apparatuses.[11] And it would remain the province of a minority much smaller than even Leavis imagined. In effect, criticism after the modernist epoch, despite its reformist impulse, will be an esoteric craft compelled to demonstrate literature's social and experiential strength in terms that accommodate themselves to a society for which its purposes are either meaningless, obsolete, or dangerously illiberal, a society for which, in turn, criticism can have no compelling respect.

To conceive of literary criticism like this is, once again, to return to the spirit of the paragraphs that closed the previous chapter and to echo Leo Strauss's view that philosophers qua philosophers cannot wholly belong to their society because they must think outside the presuppositions and beliefs that enable social stability. But it is not that literary critics, like Strauss's philosophers, need to believe too little to be wholly socialized; on the contrary, they need to believe too much. We can recall that Eliot once wrote, "It takes application, and a kind of genius, to believe *anything*" (quoted in Leavis 1962, 90). Nonetheless, Strauss's insistence on the distance between philosophy and society do help us imagine the future of literary criticism as a tiny, beleaguered, and disregarded sect devoted to poetic or fictional articulations, recollections, or intimations of more perfect experiences. And I say this despite having no regard for Strauss's own reactionary notion of "liberal education," which shows no understanding of why the positive concepts that Strauss invokes—notably, à la Cardinal Newman, "education to perfect gentlemanliness"—became obsolete during the violent emergence of democratic state capitalism, being in large part pushed aside by the categories of experience and historicity, as we've seen (Strauss 1995, 6). But of all the academic intellectuals who worked in the modernist era, Strauss retained the strongest *corporate* sense of the consequences of thinking against the times.[12]

FIVE

The Literary Origins of Modern Democracy

It was in the 1830s that it first became clear that, come what may, democracy would ultimately triumph over its enemies. That was also the last decade in which it was still possible to think cogently of European democracy apart from industrial capitalism. In this chapter, I want to explore certain relations between literature (understood broadly) and this sense that history was taking a new and irrevocable turn.

By the 1830s, it had long been recognized that modern democracy contained three separate drives, each broadcast in the French revolutionary publicity machines after 1789: (1) liberty (or freedom), (2) equality, and (3) fraternity (or, more weakly, communal solidarity and participation). To these we may immediately add the Rousseauian and Jacobin concept of "popular sovereignty" (in which, as Rousseau put it, the people and the sovereign are identical), which, by around 1830, was seen to distinguish a democratic from a republican constitution (Rousseau 1973, 29). The nineteenth-century reception of the democratic ideal was characterized by a deepening understanding that these four drives were in fact heterogeneous. By the century's end, for instance, William Lecky could argue not just that liberty and equality might under some circumstances be in tension but that, as the histories of the Roman and the French (post-1789) republics demonstrated, they were incompatible (Lecky 1981, 1:22ff.).[1] And the critique inaugurated in Benjamin Constant's enunciation of a liberalism distinct from republicanism, after Constant realized that individual liberty could be doubly threatened by the institutionalization of the general will and the new commercial society, had by the 1880s developed into a profound standoff between liberalism and social democracy, especially in Britain (see Constant 1988; for the "new liberalism," see Collini 1993 and Clarke 1978).

Yet equality, collectivism, popular sovereignty, and liberty had already come adrift by the 1830s. We can put it like this: in its early stages, the historical and enlightened struggle for democracy had predominantly figured itself as emancipatory, as a struggle for freedom against arbitrary, corrupt, and repressive privilege and authority. (For a similar point, see Schmitt 1985, 15–16.) But once the political legitimacy of modern liberty was granted (we can think of the 1830 European revolutions and in Britain the 1832 Reform Act as sealing this legitimacy), democracy was slowly implemented under the still more contentious signs of popular sovereignty and equality.[2] At that point, the distance between the practical outcomes of constitutions set in place by popular sovereignty and the people's actual wants and needs was recognized—first in the 1830s, by the early socialists and by the rightist French Catholic priest Félicité Lamennais, and a couple of decades or so later by Marxist revolutionaries.[3] Up until the middle of the twentieth century, these separate democratic drives remained loosely attached to different classes: liberty was basically a bourgeois standard; equality and popular sovereignty (whether constitutional or not) were working-class ones. That class struggle continued, sometimes merely fitfully, until about 1968, when the proletariat's claims to be an agent of democratic emancipation stalled for good. As a result, democracy was again transformed, becoming practically rather than theoretically unsurpassable and, as unsurpassable, effectively marking a limit to the history of emancipation as such, for better or for worse. As the young Marx had put it, democracy at last became the "truth" of all state politics whatsoever (see Marx 1985, 89).

Alexis de Tocqueville

Indubitably the most important text of the moment when democracy became known as "predestined fate" (Mannheim 1956, 171) was Alexis de Tocqueville's *Democracy in America*, the first volume of which appeared in 1835 and the second in 1840. Committed to prophecy, mixing speculation with careful, quasi-novelistic observation, *Democracy in America* predicts democracy's advent in Europe while aiming to help Europe—France in particular—recognize and prepare for the dangers of democracy.[4]

Three points about Tocqueville's profoundly influential intervention need to be made immediately.

First, his book is a literary text as much as it is a sociological one (to use a term unavailable to Tocqueville himself). This is to say that, for all his ethnographic care, Tocqueville here *imagines* democracy as much as he describes and analyzes it. And he takes a position toward democracy that is not quite consistent or fully spelled out but that we can describe as friendly criticism (or perhaps, in the second volume especially, intimate enmity). *Democracy in America* helps create democracy from the point of view of a liberal aristocrat who wishes to conserve order and stability: a conservative liberal in the lineage of Montesquieu and Burke. So Tocqueville, for instance, resisted the franchise's extension in Britain after 1832 and became, at best, a defender of a form of guardian or *garantiste* democracy, in which the state protects itself against full political democracy in the perceived interests of civil society as a whole.[5] Indeed, in his later study of the French ancien régime, Tocqueville would come to argue against progressivism as such, contending that the condition of the French peasantry was better in the fifteenth century than in modern times under state centralization (Tocqueville 1955, 146–147).

Second, *Democracy in America* has no truck with the most philosophical contemporary schools of political theory. It has no truck, in particular, with the German idealism that then dominated European thought, including an influential contemporary contribution to the debate, Coleridge's *Constitution of Church and State* (1830). And it is written in implicit renunciation of the contemporary surge of utopian socialism in France associated with Saint-Simon, Enfantin, Bazard, and Comte, a spiritual faith in the efficacy of love of a unified humanity, which came to be called "the religion of humanity" or, in some forms, "mystical democracy" and to which we will return in the next chapter.[6]

Third, Tocqueville does not recognize capitalism as a specific form of social organization. Hence the crucial question of what in America flows from democracy and what flows from capitalism is not explicitly addressed. But it's useful to remember in this regard that an analyst such as Joseph Schumpeter, writing a century after Tocqueville, could make arguments very similar to his but now about capitalism rather than democracy (see Schumpeter 1950, 121–130).

Tocqueville is primarily concerned with equality rather than with fraternity or freedom (Tocqueville 1966, 3). As he argues, egalitarianism is the form of democracy that Americans have chosen because it requires the least personal sacrifice of them (49, 475). And he does not have a substantive understanding of equality. He does not, for instance, share the enlightened belief of Descartes and Helvétius that all human beings possess equal capabilities by nature: Descartes famously begins his *Discours de la méthode* (1637) with the observation that "*Le bon sens est la chose du monde la mieux partagée*," an (admittedly Thomist) proto–cultural democratic phrase that does as well as any other to set off the political project of the Enlightenment. Nor is equality to be found in civic virtue (*arête*) or the duty to die for one's country in battle, as it was in Athenian democracy (see Schmitt 1985, 9). Nor in a moral anthropology based on shared emotional nature—on Bernard Williams's capacity to suffer, for example (Williams 2007). Or on our shared vulnerability to force and domination, as Simone Weil believed. Tocqueville does not even view equality as the liberal right to participate in a democratic polity committed to, in Laski's phrase, the politics of discussion and openness (Laski 1921, 66). For that reason, he had little interest, in particular, in using the education system to develop citizens' capacities to participate in self-government. Rather, American democracy is established upon a successful will to implement "equality of conditions," a phrase that obscures as much as it clarifies but that we might understand as assuming the merely categorical equality that underpins the drive for the relatively even distribution of the resources (that is, "conditions") that are required for anyone to enter into American life on their own terms. For Tocqueville, as for more committed democrats, we are equal and have a claim to the fulfillment of that fundamental equality because we are human beings and not because we are equal in any substantive sense.

Actually, this is to make too large a claim on Tocqueville's view of American democracy, since he insists that in practice such equality only covers the white settlers and their descendants. This is not because he himself acceded to the notion of radical superiority but because he believed, as a matter of fact, that native Americans had not been accommodated into settler society and were hence headed to extermination (Tocqueville 1966, 312), and because he also believed that African Americans, subject to intolerance and "exposed to the tyranny of laws," were doomed to becoming "unlucky remnants" in the nation. "Nothing but the injustices and hardships to which they are subjected will call attention to their presence" (322–323), he wrongly predicted, in an implicitly damning judgment on American democracy's capacity to secure social justice.

For our purposes, however, what is of most interest in Tocqueville is not his concept of equality as such but his grasp of how democratization shapes society and culture generally. In American democracy, he argues, equality achieves "dominion over civil society as much as government" (3). Or, as Pierre Manent puts it, in Tocqueville democracy becomes "the horizon of all undertakings"; it takes hold of its people's "entire life" (Manent 1996, 9). Fundamental democracy, in short. Yet again, it's a little more complicated than this, since democracy operates in two directions simultaneously. It denotes not just the implementation of equal conditions across all social and cultural domains but also the shaping power on political processes of the American settler colony's already informally democratized *moeurs*, to use Tocqueville's term for what we might rather call *ethos*.

What then, in more detail, does Tocqueville observe in America? For him, it seems, American democracy cannot be considered separately from America's amazing prosperity, although this prosperity is more a result of the continent's geography, of the available possibilities for primitive accumulation, and of the historical motives for its European settlement than of its Constitution. The opportunities that flow from this prosperity combine with democratization to encourage an overriding materialism, individualism, and instrumentalism. America aims at worldly well-being; it does not encourage aspirations toward what might lie beyond the world. Spiritually and philosophically, democracy flattens horizons: it tends to a dangerous Spinozan pantheism (Tocqueville 1966, 417–418), the very same danger of which Pierre Lasserre was later to warn. While religion prospers in America, it does so merely as a necessary, if restricted because privatized, source of counterdemocratic morality, which can partly recompense for the disappearance of unified and hierarchical society (516–517). In secular life, a similar foreshortening is apparent. It is true, for instance, that at a national level America is obsessed with "military glory" (256), but this drive to elevation is curtailed. Compassion flourishes (535), and social interactions are easy, relaxed (539). It is a regime of conversational democracy. In public life, traditions and distinctions disappear, as does good taste (451)—victims too of the loss of stability, leisure, and rank. As such, indeed, it is a regime of cultural democracy, although, of course, Tocqueville does not himself assent to this cultural democracy in any unqualified manner. Indeed, as Sheldon Wolin has noticed, he is particularly sensitive to the democratic threat to individual "greatness" and organic solidarity that remains in place in Europe, if precariously now that democracy is imminent there (Wolin 2003, 121).

For Tocqueville, America is also ceaselessly mobile, under "permanent agitation" (Tocqueville 1966, 427) just by virtue of the forces that propel American democracy to the ordinary, the earthly, the prosperous, and the practical. This mobility has its dark side: stripped of any secure inherited place in communities, Americans are doomed both to social isolation ("each man is thrown back on his own," 478) and to "impatient longing" (454), a socially caused intensification of that "uneasiness" that seemed experience's default setting to Saint Augustine as well as to John Locke at the beginning of political modernity. In a word, what lies at democratic America's heart is a dynamic instability that inhabits an uncontested ordinariness and rips individual lives from their social settings and limits.

Democracy's unstable, anxious, yet gentle individualism is counterbalanced by a public opinion that imposes itself to such an extent that it can be considered sovereign. Actually, public opinion does not exactly *counter* democracy's dangerous dynamism; it overshadows and squashes it. Tocqueville views public opinion as an externalized general will whose power exceeds that of formal political relations so that American popular sovereignty becomes in effect the sovereignty of agglutinated collective belief. Therefore, for all democracy's encouragement of individualism and isolation, at this point equality becomes uniformity. By suppressing individual character and autonomy, public opinion in effect creates a serialized society of individuals, mimetic of one or another, each of whom lacks singularity and distinction.

Politically, democracy is threatened from within on various fronts. Most important (and famously), it enables a new form of tyranny—that of the majority. And Tocqueville emphasizes the various ways in which America protects itself—must protect itself—against majoritarian despotism. Also, America is structurally prone to a monstrous reoligarchization, since industrialization and free-market principles, when combined with formal equality of conditions, are likely to create a new class of the rich, a perverse plebeian ruling caste who possess neither internal solidarity (that is, any sense of caste specificity) nor an institutional or historic sense of responsibility to the poor (529). And, despite the saving strength of its local governments and associations, America is also threatened by a drastic extension and empowerment of a paternalistic centralized state (familiar enough to Tocqueville in France), which, when it takes a democratic form, may come to "relieve" its citizens "from the trouble of thinking and all the cares of living" (667).

Implicit in this account of American democracy, with its reliance on paradox, lies a sociological claim with metaphysical implications that we can formularize like this: in American democracy, experience counts for more than in Europe. What Tocqueville finally admires about the "people in the United States" is their "experience and good sense" (279–280). In part, experience (admittedly more as a concept than as a word) comes to the fore for methodological reasons. As noted above, it is what remains in democratic life as tradition and distinction retreat. Tocqueville's dual impulse to theory and empiricism is rhetorically at least reconciled in his thick descriptions of how anyone lives in America, a mode of literary-phenomenological abstraction that, as he seems to concede, is itself a fruit of democratization, because of his sense that it is actual ways of life, or rather the experiences that these ways of life nurture, which propel democracy forward (450).

So experience matters to American democracy just because democracy's instability and materialist instrumentalism grant preeminent value to a kind of Aristotelian *phronesis*. In earlier conservative thought—that is, in Burke—experience was aligned to traditional society *against* theory, since experience, affirmatively parsed as prejudice, was shaped by stabilizing inherited social structures. But now the opposite is true. According to Tocqueville, Americans "neglect theory" and give up on the "divine love of truth" for practical knowledge (429). Experience is cast adrift from institutions and norms in place and thrown into the play between modern commerce, the democratic state, and civil society. This helps explain why democratic experience in Tocqueville's account is already divided and ambiguous. It denotes a relation to the world that is both more concrete and more abstract than traditional experience; it is more self-enclosed, uneasy, and selfish as well as more open. As I say, it is more restless but also more corporeal and "earthward" (422).

One sees this even in his treatment of the topic that most concerns us—in his prophecies of literature's own fate in America. According to Tocqueville, only aristocratic societies can create and sustain literary autonomy, which he thought of as understanding of literature "as an art," loving it "for its own sake," and taking "a scholarly pleasure that the rules are obeyed" (439). On the other hand, Americans, who share no identity, who lack grandeur and singularity, will read works designed "to astonish more than to please, and to stir passions rather than to charm taste" (441). Democratic literature will also aim at transparency and worldliness: it will avoid allegory and figures, will "not feed on legends or on traditions and memories," and will not "people the universe again with supernatural beings" (455). Rather, it will *realistically* describe and seek to comprehend human nature in general.

In other words, it will be experientially based, just like *Democracy in America* itself, and aim to extend representation to the limits of pantheist immanentism:

> [Man] himself not tied to time and place, but face to face with nature and with God, with his passions, his doubts, his unexpected good fortune, and his incomprehensible miseries, will for these people be the chief and almost the sole subject of poetry. One can already be sure that this will be so if one considers the greatest poets that have appeared in the world since it turned towards democracy. (455)

It's an insight that seems to predict literary projects like Walt Whitman's or Herman Melville's as expressed, for instance, in Melville's manifesto for democratic writing in *Moby Dick*:

> But this august dignity I treat of, is not the dignity of kings and robes, but that abounding dignity which has no robed investiture. Thou shalt see it shining in the arm that wields a pick or drives a spike; that democratic dignity which, on all hands, radiates without end from God; Himself! The great God absolute! The centre and circumference of all democracy! His omnipresence, our divine equality!
>
> If, then, to meanest mariners, and renegades and castaways, I shall hereafter ascribe high qualities, though dark; weave around them tragic graces; if even

> the most mournful, perchance the most abased, among them all, shall at times lift himself to the exalted mounts; if I shall touch that workman's arm with some ethereal light; if I shall spread a rainbow over his disastrous set of sun; then against all mortal critics bear me out in it, thou just Spirit of Equality, which hast spread one royal mantle of humanity over all my kind! (Melville 2008, 102)

Here "nobility" becomes "dignity," which is, in turn, an emanation of a profoundly political and egalitarian divinity embodied and revealed in the people, even in abased criminals and slaves. It is as pure an expression of political pantheism as we are likely to find. But Melville is writing this more than a decade after Tocqueville, for whom, in the end, the "greatest poets that have appeared in the world since it turned to democracy" have a different complexion.

Tocqueville himself thinks of the Byron of *Childe Harold*, the Chateaubriand of *Renée*, and the Lamartine who created Jocelyn in *Les Visions* as the democratic writers par excellence of his time. For him, these are not, as they have often been understood, romantic figures concerned to assert greatness or originality of spirit in a mechanistic world, warriors against what Byron called the "craving void," or lyricists of a equality's dark "high qualities," but rather expressions of universalizing democratized humanism suffused by existential anxiety (Byron 1974, 3:109). Tocqueville is here closer to Kojève's reading of Byron as Hegel's literary equivalent, who introduces literature to history's end by revealing that henceforth heroism would be purely peaceful and civil (Kojève 1956, 702–703). However, from a requisite distance these various understandings of where and how democracy and literature intersect with the other turn out to be versions of one another just because Tocqueville's socialized anxiety and unpredictability, Melville's divinely abject dignity, and Byronic individuated, rather ersatz, heroism are produced from the same sources, from democracy's unmooring of experience from solid social foundations and its submersion of experience and personhood in the uneasy, horizontal sublimities of equality and immanence.

In sum, Tocqueville invents—or imagines—a prophetic, wide-ranging, complex, internally divided democratic anthropology that provides a template for understanding how democracy and the democratic experience work on culture and that, as we will see, will remain difficult to move beyond right into the present.

Benjamin Disraeli

Let us now turn to very different account of democracy in the period, one that is more literary still. In 1835, the then would-be politician Benjamin Disraeli wrote a series of polemical pieces that, for all their glibness, carelessness with facts, and sheer opportunism, spell out an original theory of, and program for, British democracy. Disraeli would extend this theory in *Coningsby* and *Sybil*, the first two volumes of his 1840s "condition of England" novel trilogy, in which he, unlike Tocqueville, comes to terms with the social impact of industrialization and the emergence of an urban industrial proletariat. These texts are not exactly opposed to Tocqueville's findings and judgments, but they point in a different direction, since Disraeli does not so much search for limits to, and protection from, democratization as assert that democratization may reinvigorate its opposite.[7] Democracy is treated as an ecology in which antidemocratic conservatism may flourish. Because he grasped that continually surprising truth, Disraeli too becomes a prophet of the counter-Enlightenment grip on the democratic imagination. In that role, he also points toward the various conservative communitarianisms or "socialisms" that dominated Europe in the first half of the twentieth century, of which probably the most theoretically compelling was Maurrassian/Sorelian "integral nationalism"; the most chilling, of course, was realized in Hitler's Germany.[8]

On the other side, Disraeli intuits that the left's rationalist, proceduralist, or constitutional politics circle around an empty center, since they lack a concrete, imaginative vision of the good society. That is why he believed that conservatives were well equipped to succeed under the new constitution. They could persuasively project the promise of a well-ordered society, a civic imaginary as we can call it, into the public world and hence need not despair of competing on the new democratic terrain.

So like Tocqueville, if more happily, Disraeli accepts that politics will be democratized. Indeed, he became the political leader who extended the British male franchise in 1867. And in his political writings of the 1840s, Disraeli offered a historically based theory that demonstrated his faith in Tory democracy as well as providing intellectual grounds for it. It demands closer inspection.

At its heart lay the notion of "equality of civil rights," or what Disraeli sometimes called "civic equality" (Disraeli 1913, 228–229). These were the rights, embedded both in common law and in inherited institutions and customs, that allowed all British subjects to participate in civil society, securely to own property, and not to be subject to arbitrary arrest. As such, they guaranteed the constitutional grounds for all to make careers and to achieve prosperity for themselves (161). Thus Disraeli as a politician passed important labor laws that helped Britain toward a somewhat gentler capitalism than that which would exist in the United States, for instance—the Conspiracy and Protection of Property Act (1875), which guaranteed the right to strike; and the Employers and Workmen Act (1875), which supported worker's rights in their contracts with employers. Civic equality also underpinned the peculiarly English freedom of passage from the aristocracy to the bourgeoisie and back, which created a new kind of social personality and style, the "gentleman," who, so Disraeli contended, helps guarantee the national social system's stability. This, at any rate, was an equality that elevated rather than leveled, in Disraeli's own epigrammatic phrase (229). Importantly, this notion of democracy meant that Disraelian democracy, unlike Tocqueville's, was essentially national. It could not be transferred to other nation-states. And it also meant that real democracy was *not* in the service of those social reformers like the utilitarians, whose calculations weakened substantive notions of the communal good. For Disraeli, democracy was inherited. It was not realized by modernizing, rationalizing governments. For him, that kind of government ended up working on behalf of an oligarchy, just as Tocqueville feared.

It was for these reasons that Disraeli was convinced that devout democrats should be familiar with their national pasts, and his political theory itself was largely devoted to sketching out a revisionist account of modern English history.[9] That account pivoted on the struggle between Whigs and Tories, which, following Bolingbroke, Disraeli believed to have structured English history from the Reformation on, if not earlier.[10] He argues that the Whigs took advantage of the material opportunities opened up by Henry VIII's despoliation of the monasteries to privatize much of the country's land. In the late seventeenth century, they went on to establish the institutions that created public debt and finance capitalism. Now they were manipulating the utilitarian reformers for their own ends, responsible for the immiseration caused by the Poor Law Amendment Act (1834) and its incarceration of the indigent unemployed, for instance. In short, they were republicans and oligarchs who had imposed a "Venetian polity" upon

England, transforming the sovereign into a doge. It was their opponents, the Tories, who were the true democrats and defenders of civic equality (337)—they had resisted both the Reformation and rampant capitalism, and with Bolingbroke, Burke, Shelburne, and Pitt had developed theories and policies that were capable of resisting modernizing social breakdown and that might implement a new spiritual compact between monarch and multitude.

More specifically, English equality of civil rights provided the basis for a corporate nation to be imagined and instituted; it is precisely because such rights exist that equality need not cover society in all its institutions and zones. Disraeli's English society is divided into estates—the aristocracy, the bourgeoisie, the Church, and laborers—none of whom can claim to be *the* people and each of whom has different functions, responsibilities, and privileges. According to Disraeli, popular sovereignty involves a misapprehension, since the people as such cannot be represented—the very concept "people" is a figment of "political science," he claimed, and by the late 1840s he was routinely using the term "multitude" instead (see Disraeli 1927, 8:39 for the citation; Disraeli 1853 for "multitude"). Indeed, government is essentially "irresponsible," since it cannot be bound to the will of any specific interest or constituency, while no constituency can represent every subject of the nation (44–49). The multitude, organized into estates, acquires equality not through participation in government but just through belonging to the nation.

Of the various estates, only the bourgeoisie have or need access to the politics of electoral representation: "Representation is not . . . in a principal sense Parliamentary," as Coningsby put it (Disraeli 1913, 8:375). That is to say, most forms of social representation are (as Burke put it) virtual (Burke 1990). For instance, the sovereign represents the nation outside of the mechanics of electoral politics, and the clergy and aristocracy represent the rural poor not through electoral representation but because they had charge of what Disraeli called the "parochial constitution" (that is, parish administration, through which England was still largely governed), and they do so through their obligated but not, in the modern sense, wholly private and individual ownership of the land.[11] Under such a regime of virtual representation, the state's interests were managed by politicians with a flair for high politics—largely centered on foreign affairs—while civil society more largely was governed through local associations, institutions, and customs.

The last strut of Disraeli's appropriation of democracy for English conservatism was theopolitical, although by the end of his life he believed that this theopolitics had been irredeemably betrayed by Anglican ritualism and John Henry Newman's conversion to Catholicism. As we have seen, he argued that Whiggism was the long-term sociopolitical consequence of the Reformation and then, further, that Toryism, vulnerable under Whig domination, had been formed and kept alive by the Anglican country clergy, heirs of the victims of the Church's sacking under Henry VIII and who, of course, possessed an immediate, and so to say expressive, relation to the English rural poor through their pastoral services. More than that, the clergy were filiatively connected not just to apostolic succession but to Israel's prophets, who typologically foretold Christ's coming. So there's a sense that monarchical and corporate nationalism is, for Disraeli, based on—or at least intimately associated with—an Anglo-Catholic ecclesiology itself ultimately dependent on divine revelations that extend back to ancient Judaism and through which the contemporary Semite and Arab world and their theocratic traditions resonate with that of English democracy. This imaginative theopolitics is spelled out most fully in the third volume of Disraeli's trilogy, *Tancred* (1847), in which a Byronic, existentially anxious, eponymous hero finds personal stability by traveling to the Near East in search of the sources of faith and falling in love with a young Jewish woman in Jerusalem.

In his 1840s trilogy—*Coningsby*, *Sybil*, and *Tancred*—Disraeli's attempt to align democracy to a Tory civic imaginary undergoes a number of modifications. Each novel is a bildungsroman telling a story of a young English aristocrat who notices crippling insufficiencies in English society and polity and who, in seeking to remit them, comes to accept a version of the Tory-democratic interpretation of history before at last finding a resolution to his search by marrying a woman from outside his class. Disraeli's heroes, that is, learn that a new political movement or project is required to break with the long period of Whig hegemony, given the Tory failure under Sir Robert Peel to spell out a counterprogram to Whiggishness. In the trilogy's first two volumes at least, the new Toryism will be based on principles. It will also have a strong sense of exactly what in England needs to be conserved and will know how what is to be conserved is to be reorganized so as to bend the social transformations consequent upon industrialization into a coherent polity. But most important (to use our own terms rather than Disraeli's), it will construct a civic imaginary able to command public opinion.

In the trilogy, the world of formal politics—"high politics"—is only loosely connected to the world of "low politics," that is, the politics that express actual social interests beyond Westminster.[12] In the first two volumes, further, this critique of political manners is inserted into a split historical temporality. The novels' actions take place against the flow of recent political events; Peel and Wellington's 1829 passage of Catholic emancipation (the Catholic Relief Act); the 1832 Reform Act; the 1834 Poor Law Amendment Act; the 1837 coronation of Queen Victoria, that year's general election, and the jockeying for power that followed; Peel's procapitalist policies and repeal of the Corn Laws in 1846. It's a sequence that would transform Tory politics and create the scenario for Disraeli's rise to power alongside the defeat of Chartism and, with it, intensify the English will to popular, rather than parliamentary, sovereignty. On another level, though, the accession of the novel's aristocratic families to their land and status is recorded in relation to the long *durée* of Whig hegemony that had already been outlined in his earlier political writing. Hence the fact that the Marney family in *Sybil* acquired their estate from Henry VIII's seizure of the monasteries fixes their function in English society and makes sense of their current modish, utilitarian indifference to plebeian suffering.

So Disraeli registers the impoverishment and insecurity of the industrial proletariat and seeks to ameliorate them without turning to reform as the philosophical radicals understood it. In particular, he does not advocate either state centralization or popular education. Instead, he urges that Erastian relations between the Church and state be terminated, and that the Church should be constitutionally independent of government. The Church's contribution to English culture should be properly acknowledged. It should be adequately financed so that it can rebuild the infrastructure required for it to take charge of the people's spiritual and material welfare. On that basis, the parochial constitution and a pastorally inclined leadership could be applied to industrial factories—that's the message of Trafford's happy factory in *Sybil*. Furthermore, in the spirit of Bolingbrokean patriotism, Disraeli urges that a strong national leader will be required, probably but not necessarily the monarch—there's room for Caesarism in Disraeli's early political theory, as the young Hegelian, Bruno Bauer, long ago pointed out (Bauer 1882, 51). Charismatic, nonrepresentative leadership can resist oligarchies and operate in the interest of the people as a whole, since, as Tocqueville also remarked, absolutism can be more egalitarian than republicanism. In alliance with the Church and inspired youth, a charismatic sovereign could also, Disraeli implies, persuasively communicate a counter-Enlightenment social vision.

At the same time, Disraeli embraces the concept of race. For him, race is an egalitarian concept: there's a sense in which membership of a race confers formal internal equality so that a racially limited "natural aristocracy" can emerge from within a race quite unlike the debased and parasitic Whig oligarchy (Disraeli 1927, 8:178). But race is also a concept that separates. In *Sybil*, there are hints that the adversaries that constitute modern British politics are based in an older racial colonialist struggle: the one between Saxons and Normans in England (9:206). (This, of course, is the famous "Norman yoke" theory of British history.) More to the point, however, it is the Jews, whom, as "Semites," Disraeli does not distinguish from the Arabs, who are different from other races.[13] That's because they are closer to God, and the ancient Jewish polity developed under God's command, which remains residually in place in the Arabian deserts and survives as the historic source of sanctioned social hierarchy. This Semitic polity may acquire a renewed influence in modern Europe, as the Jewish finance capitalist and omniscient intellectual Sidonia, a Rothschild-like figure, attests in *Coningsby* (8:266–267).

In the first two volumes of the trilogy, Disraeli also extends his theory of virtual representation. Now his belief that the monarch, landed gentry, and clergy can, as it were, cover for the laborers and the poor has weakened. Only the clergy retains vestiges of that capacity. Indeed, the novels show how the opportunistic embrace of philosophical radicalism by Whig magnates like *Sybil*'s Lord Marney cause starvation and misery and so foment Chartism, incendiarism, and a fierce will to popular sovereignty. The new vehicle of virtual representation, which offsets revolutionary energies, is the media itself. The free press will circulate all opinions, including those principles and images that will be required to revive conservatism, such as Disraeli's own writings. It's an arena where the political and cultural advantage of conservatism over rationalist politics can be played out. At the same time, it's the free press that will most effectively represent the people outside the reductive mechanisms of parliamentary democracy. Indeed, such democracy is already mediatized: elections may be won or lost on what Disraeli calls "cries," publicized slogans on behalf of a particular party or candidate.

In *Tancred*, the stakes for democracy are raised. It is in fact another prophetic, if fantastic, text. Tancred comes to believe that effective resistance to the social extension of enlightened, instrumental rationality and the ideology of progress upon which it depends requires a move beyond politics, nothing less than a return to monotheism's sources, that is, to the desert. This enables the novel to turn to a different, more confessionally aware inflection of post-Enlightenment political Spinozism than Melville's, say, one designed to reconcile Jew and Christian. Which is to say that it embraces a political theology most fully spelled out by another young Hegelian, Moses Hess, who wished to overcome Christianity's enmity with Judaism first by assigning both faiths to the same mental faculties and then by making ambitious claims for those faculties: "Faith is the foundation of knowledge just as fantasy is the foundation of reason" (Hess 2004, 46). Doctrine and revelation are here seconded to a particular imaginative energy shared by Christians and Jews alike, whose most profound creation is monotheism, and that today might triumph over confessional and political difference and, thence, over liberalism, which, from Hess's perspective, accedes to a kind of political polytheism.

Disraeli's Tancred sets out for the Near East. After a night's vigil at the Church of the Holy Sepulcher in Jerusalem, he becomes convinced of the power of "theocratic equality" (378)—equality among those who worship the one true God of the deserts, a God whom Jews, Christians, and Muslims share. His quest for faith is also a political quest, then. Theocratic equality is a simultaneously social and devotional equality, which, since it sacralizes monarchical sovereignty, does not interrupt social hierarchy; indeed, it does not interrupt feudalism itself. In fact, it points forward to the conjunction between monarchism and popular nationalism preached in the earlier volumes and that Disraeli was to achieve as a Tory leader but that (as we have seen) was to fail Action Française in twentieth-century France. Here it reveals itself within the theater of empire. Tancred comes to believe that Europe will "fall in love" with Asia, as the territory where God becomes present to the world, while Asia in its turn will fall in love with Europe, because Europe retains a "steadfast and commanding spirit" (Disraeli 1927, 10:264) that Asia has lost. In their passion for each other, Asia is to "save Europe" (10:318). This belief encourages Tancred's fantasies of an imperialism in reverse. He hopes to raise an army in Syria and Lebanon in order to conquer the secular West on behalf of true religion and polity. But, for the novel, the hard business of political maneuvering, manipulation, and negotiation can be carried out only by the self-interested, obsessed intriguer Fakredeen, emir of Lebanon, a strange mixture of enthusiast and cynic. Fakredeen's schemes fail, and at the novel's ambiguous and incomplete end, Tancred seems rather to settle for a private life of exile in Jerusalem with a beautiful Jewish girl.

This is, as I say, a fantastic story. And when Disraeli communicates his message through fiction, then a new relationship enters visibility: that between the politics of explicit democratization and the novel form itself. I have been arguing that Disraeli embraces democracy while rejecting most of the principles and institutions that were organizing and implementing actual political democratization in his time. In choosing the novel form as he inherited it to communicate his message, he exposes it to this divided political will. He democratizes the novel genre at the same time that he Toryizes or aristocraticizes it. He also demonstrates, in effect if not intentionally, how the novel form's generic features map onto the terrain in which democratization was a political stake.

Let's backtrack a little to help us examine how this works. Disraeli began his public career as a writer of fashionable novels and achieved considerable success with his first, *Vivian Grey* (1827). This is sometimes classed as a "silver-fork" novel (that is, a novel set among a fashionable metropolitan society that it simultaneously satirizes and spectacularizes). But that description is not quite accurate: *Vivian Grey* is rather another truncated bildungs roman, which charts the gradual maturation of its preternaturally cynical and manipulative young hero. The first volume is set in England and involves Vivian's leadership of a political intrigue (which refers to real political events): an attempt to create a new parliamentary group under the nominal charge of a complacent peer. But his scheming comes to nothing. Vivian suffers a moral collapse and departs to Heidelberg, whose court and *moeurs* are described inside the conventions of popular German romanticism, then at the height of its literary fashion. It's a fiction where what matters is not the characters' moral personalities, not their interiorities, not their affective responsiveness to the ordinary and contingent, not sympathy's attractions and risks, not their experiences qua experiences, not even (as in the silver-fork novel proper) their sumptuary styles and deportment, but rather the actual social possibilities for Byronic ambition. Indeed, Vivian's career is worth attending to for two more particular reasons: his careerist cynicism looks forward to Disraeli's later characters like *Tancred*'s Fakredeen and to Disraeli's own public reputation as a political adventurer and hired voice. If the English landed aristocracy had not then needed a brilliant rhetorician and strategist, Disraeli would have become "another Lassalle," as Schumpeter remarked (Schumpeter 1950, 229). Vivian's story, cloaked in fictionality, functions then as uncannily proleptic autocritique, a preemptive deployment of self-awareness to deflect criticism of the opportunism more or less imposed upon Disraeli by the fact that he was born the child of a London Jewish man of letters. But more important, the failure of Vivian's political scheming points to parliamentary politics' failure to connect to society's interests—it articulates an empty space between parliament and society—that is, to that absence which stimulates the will to political democracy and which conservatism as embodied in Disraeli's trilogy can best occupy.

At any rate, Disraeli brings elements of his experiment with *Vivian Grey* to his political novels of the 1840s, where the scheming, self-interested world of party politics, Whig *and* Tory, is opened to fascinated and pointed mockery. It is viewed as all but irrelevant to the world of the industrial proletariat, into which Disraeli, along with Mrs. Gaskell and others, had extended the novel's mimetic range. But it's not this extension that matters most to us. Disraeli's will to democratize expresses itself most powerfully in literary terms through his application of conversational democracy. By this I mean his fictional representation of equal social exchanges across class and other hierarchies. And, contrariwise, his resistance to democratization is most powerful in the absence of representations of democratic experience and feeling in his fictions, an absence we can interpret as a refusal of democratization thought in terms of political equality, which is also, ultimately, a refusal of the genealogy of sensibility that nurtured democratic experience in the English novel before the establishment of political democracy itself.

The evidence for these propositions is best found in *Sybil*, where Disraeli's English social range is widest. Take the scene in the first volume where, late one afternoon, the novel's hero, Egremont, Lord Marney's younger brother, encounters two strangers, Walter Gerard and Stephen Morely, at a cemetery attached to a ruined abbey on his family estate. In the novel's own social taxonomy, these strangers turn out to be workers, albeit what we would now call white-collar workers. It's a scene of a contingent encounter with social inferiors structurally similar to many in sentimental literature: Laurence Sterne's *A Sentimental Journey* basically consists of a series of just such encounters.

In Sterne, what is most important is the serial solicitation of experiences and especially emotional response (of either intense compassion or light eroticism, or both) to the degree that setting and the characters' bodies are all but absent as material objects in his novels, existing rather as vibrations or nerves, experience's barely material vehicles. And Sterne's sentimental encounters often end in an act of private charity of no clear political import.

Here it is very different. Egremont is deep in thought when he first meets the strangers, and he is deliberating social injustice and its historical causes:

> Why were these hard times for the poor? He stood among the ruins that . . . had seen many changes: changes of creeds, of dynasties, of laws, of manners. New orders of men had arisen in the country, new sources of wealth had opened, new dispositions of power to which that wealth had necessarily led. His own house, his own order, had established themselves on the ruins of that great body, the emblems of whose ancient magnificence and strength surrounded him. And now his order was in turn menaced. (Disraeli 1927, 9:69)

At this point, Egremont notices two strangers near him, the elder of whose physical appearance is immediately presented in an abstract, utterly conventional description in which the body represents a moral self. The stranger has "a frank and manly countenance," his "features were regular and handsome, a well-formed nose, the square mouth and its white teeth, and the clear grey eye, which befitted such an idiosyncrasy" (70). Yet this narratorial emphasis on externalities, which seems to come from the society novel, possesses here a simultaneously racial and democratic force. As we will learn, these are *Saxon* bodies as conceived in that populist historiography that regarded the English people as descendants of the Saxons, and their rulers as descendants of the Normans. *That* is why what counts here is bodies and, by the same stroke, character rather than social status.

This abstract description of objects anchors what is ultimately an irreal scene—since in the real world of 1840 the son of an earl would not likely engage a worker as an equal. It's on this basis that Egremont enters into a conversation with the strangers, which merely further extends his previous internal musings but in which he is quickly positioned as a pupil. He learns the Tory interpretation of history from Walter: how plebeian life on the estate was easier when the estate was owned by the monastic order and how, once it became a family's property and was available for capital improvement, conditions for the tenants and laborers worsened. At the end of Gerald's history lesson, Stephen succinctly gives the Tocquevillean moral: "There is no community in England; there is aggregation under circumstances which make it a dissolving, rather than a unifying, principle" (75).

The political point here is, of course, that Egremont is learning the truth about England from below. The social hierarchy is, for a moment and on a particular terrain, inverted. And the first literary point is that the dialogue between intellectual equals takes place in a shared dialect—that is, in a shared discursive world where the class distinctions connoted by pronunciation are elided. (Tom Nairn has claimed that phonetic variation was socially more telling in England than anywhere else in Europe; Nairn 1998, 65ff.). Indeed, this exchange sets in process a train of events that will in the end enable Egremont to marry Walter's daughter Sybil. The democratizing force of this literary moment is not spoiled by the fantastically improbable superstructure of coincidences and revelations that will also be required to sanction that marriage. It turns out that Sybil, a Saxon "natural aristocrat," is the true heir to a neighboring faux-aristocratic estate, now in possession of the descendants of a late eighteenth-century onetime waiter and Indian nabob. So in effect Egremont does not end up marrying endogamously at all. I will return to that particular break with verisimilitude, characteristic of the commercial fiction at the time, in a moment.

The more fundamental literary point is, as I say, that Egremont's encounter—like all its equivalents in Disraeli—occurs without sentimentalism. Egremont is learning the truth about England not through experience but through instruction into historical knowledge. And he feels no visceral outflows of emotion and compassion, and he does not do so even when there is greater occasion for them. He thinks and he perceives, and he *feels* merely through and in his thought and perceptions.

In the scene where he first meets Gerard and Morley, this becomes especially apparent as soon as a young woman joins them.

> At this moment a sudden flash of rosy light, suffusing the grey ruins, indicated that the sun had just fallen; and, through a vacant arch that overlooked them, alone in the resplendent sky, glittered the twilight star. The hour, the scene, the solemn stillness and the softening beauty, repressed controversy, induced even silence. The last words of the stranger lingered in the ear of Egremont; his musing spirit was teeming with many thoughts, many emotions; when from the Lady's chapel there rose the evening hymn to the Virgin. A single voice; but

> tones of almost supernatural sweetness; tender and solemn, yet flexible and thrilling.
>
> Egremont started from his reverie. He would have spoken, but he perceived that the elder of the strangers had risen from his resting-place, and, with downcast eyes and arms, was on his knees. The other remained standing in his former posture.
>
> The divine melody ceased; the elder stranger rose; the words were on the lips of Egremont, that would have asked some explanation of this sweet and holy mystery, when, in the vacant and star-lit arch on which his glance was fixed, he beheld a female form. She was apparently in the habit of a Religious, yet scarcely could be a nun, for her veil, if indeed it were a veil, had fallen on her shoulders, and revealed her thick tresses of long fair hair. The blush of deep emotion lingered on a countenance which, though extremely young, was impressed with a character of almost divine majesty; while her dark eyes and long dark lashes, contrasting with the brightness of her complexion and the luxuriance of her radiant locks, combined to produce a beauty as rare as it is choice; and so strange, that Egremont might for a moment have been pardoned for believing her a seraph, who had lighted on this sphere, or the fair phantom of some saint haunting the sacred ruins of her desecrated fane. (Disraeli 1927, 9:77–78)

What is remarkable here is precisely that Egremont does not respond to Sybil's beauty sentimentally or erotically. He barely has an experience of her. Indeed, Egremont's interiority is almost wholly evacuated largely because his response is as much intellectual as affective: he wants an explanation not just for the moment's beauty but also for its liturgical turn. Sybil is, of course, being dehumanized, spiritualized, made angelic, so that she can be figured as an allegory not so much for a relation to God as for the possibility of a binding and aesthetic religious community and calendar. She is becoming a sign of all that is not available to electoral democratization.

This argument can usefully be posed in slightly different terms: Disraeli's technique of externalization and allegory is counterdemocratic in that it does not follow Tocqueville's prophetic prescriptions for American writing: it does not represent a realist humanist experience, a mobile, mobilizing flash of feeling of one creature for another. At the passage's culminating moment, the narrator abandons Egremont's interiority for the merely conditional: "Egremont might for a moment have been pardoned." Even Sybil's "blush of deep emotion" is curiously unattached to any specific feeling. Why exactly is she blushing? Her interiority is not sufficiently available enough to us, for us to know. Angels, seraphs, ghosts of saints don't presumably have human experiences at all. Yet, for all that, it is a located moment historically, religiously, and geographically. And that locatedness subtends Disraeli's wager that what will count in the end is not availability of democratic and immanent experience but a collective imaginary, directed beyond the secular world, built out of the historically locatable ruins that have survived the processes of emancipation, egalitarianism, and rationalization.

I have said that the novel's plot, which often follows the conventions of commercial fiction, does not much affect the significance of moments within it, such as this first encounter between Egremont and the workers. But of course it is significant that Disraeli chose to circulate his diagnosis of English society in popular novel form. Presumably he made that choice because he realized, first, that in democracy, politics would be aestheticized as they invoked an imaginary collective order, and, second, that novels were a particularly effective (and profitable) vehicle for such invocations. The aesthetic construction of a politicized civic imaginary thence involved fictionalization. But fictionalizing of a Tory-democratic society through such a fantastical plot foregrounds the fact that a civic imaginary is precisely imaginary and therefore that counterdemocratic strength, in the democratic epoch, is ultimately bound to something like fictionality itself. This implicit acknowledgment of the mediation between the political and the fictional in literary terms is not to be read as irony. It's a structural effect of the conditions under which Disraeli was led to supply what was missing in the democratic process—a picture of a social end, a good, nondemocratic society—precisely in a fiction. He was making a complex political communication within a representative democracy that was also (and not coincidently) a strong—and strengthening—marketplace for novels. But the sheer fictionality of his picture of the good society meant that later novelist-critics of democracy rarely followed his example. Using more realist techniques, they tended rather to represent the travails of a privatized singularity and nobility inside democratic society, as we will see with E. M. Foster and Saul Bellow.

George Eliot

Ten years after the publication of *Tancred*, a story, "The Sad Fortunes of the Reverend Amos Barton," appeared in the Tory organ *Blackwood's Magazine* under the pseudonym George Eliot. It was later revealed that "George Eliot" was one Mary Ann Evans, who had translated the secularizing philosophers Spinoza and Feuerbach, and who was also an editor of the radical quarterly *The Westminster Review* and a member of London's most progressive intellectual circles, but who had never before published fiction. George Eliot would go on, of course, to be recognized as one of the century's most important novelists. And she was to become publicly skeptical of the democratic constitution that Disraeli had a major role in establishing, on the Tocquevillean grounds that political democracy would deliver power to the ignorant.[14] Indeed, her last novel, *Daniel Deronda* (1876), can be understood as a retelling of the *Tancred* story set in the years immediately preceding Disraeli's Second Reform Act. Like Disraeli's Tancred, its eponymous protagonist, a charismatic young man brought up on a landed estate as a country aristocrat, becomes alienated from Britain's political and social institutions, which he perceives as spiritually bankrupt. Like Tancred, he falls in love with a Jewish girl. Indeed, he becomes fascinated by Judaism and, as fate would have it, discovers that he is in fact Jewish. At the novel's end, he travels to Jerusalem with the aim of leading a Zionist movement, one founded on very different principles than secular democracy's and that loosely echo Tancred's political aspirations.

"Amos Barton," however, does not mount a spiritual critique of Britain, even if it too implicitly displaces the demand for democratic reform by religiously sanctioned emotion. The story is most remarkable for its exploration of the democratic ethos and, more particularly, for the depth and thickness of its representation of conversational democracy. It is as if it responds to Disraeli's notion that no form of democracy or liberalism can provide substantive images of, and purposes for, a good society, but it does so by turning to a very different kind of literary mimesis than Disraeli's: one based in a realism vivid, detailed, intelligent, and concrete enough to offer the illusion of readerly presence in an imagined world, a presence close to the characters' deepest interiority. Its final purpose is to elicit what we might call nonsentimental flows of moral, and fundamentally political, experience and sympathy.

"Amos Barton" is set in the period immediately prior to the Reform Act of 1832, that is, just before the triumph of democracy was widely recognized as inevitable. Its protagonist—Amos Barton—is a tactless, clumsy, charmless, poor parish curate (he has an income of eighty pounds per year), a father of six children, trying, impossibly, to raise them into the gentility expected of an Anglican clergyman. His parish is the industrializing provincial town of Shepperton, where some of the miners earn more than he does (Eliot 1900, 22). Drifting between hellfire evangelicalism and High Church Tractarianism, unable emotionally or rhetorically to connect either to his parishioners or to his fellow clergymen, organizing an unpopular "improvement" of the parish church, he muddles along. He only becomes actively ostracized when the attractive, cosmopolitan Countess Czerlaski, a pretentious and superficial young widow of an impoverished Eastern European aristocrat, who is temporarily homeless, becomes a guest in the family home. The pressure of maintaining the household while paying attention to the countess, who is insensitive and demanding, kills Amos's saintly wife, Milly, in childbirth. This leads to the novel's dénouement: Amos's genuine distress at his wife's death and his remorseful recognition of his own previous "emotional . . . poverty and selfishness" (67) causes him to be "consecrated by sorrow" and to be reconciled to the community, who offer him sympathy and charity. Nonetheless, in the end he is forced to quit Shepperton for a distant northern industrial city.

The story's narrative voice operates quite differently than does Disraeli's. It is an intimate, Fieldingesque, often chatty voice: "Reader, did you ever taste such a cup of tea as Miss Gibbs is this moment handing to Mr Pilgrim" (9). But it's also highly educated, using an idiolect only available to those socially superior to the Shepperton townspeople. Indeed, there are hints that the story is being told by a (male) clerical persona—the classical Greek citation the narrator draws upon at one point signals a dutiful university education then often associated with Anglican parsons. But for all that, the narrator (unlike Amos himself) is close to the community he describes.

Certainly the narrator (again unlike Amos) is quite open about his own social and political predilections, which are declared Tory on the first page.

> Immense improvement! says the well-regulated mind, which unintermittingly rejoices in the New Police, the Tithe Commutation Act, the penny post, and all guarantees of human advancement, and has no moments when conservative-reforming intellect takes a nap, while imagination does a little Toryism on the sly, reveling in regret that dear, old, brown, crumbling, picturesque inefficiency is everywhere giving place to spick-and-span, new-painted, new-varnished efficiency, which will yield endless diagrams, plans, elevations, and sections, but alas! no picture. Mine I fear is not a well-regulated mind: it has an occasional

> tenderness for old abuses; it lingers with a certain fondness over the days of nasal clerks and top-booted parsons, and has a sigh for the departed shades of vulgar errors. (5–6)

The tone is gently self-ironizing, yet the point of this confession—that reformist rationalism of the "conservative-reforming intellect" (that is, of Peelite conservatives, Whigs, and radicals) can only provide "diagrams," not "pictures"—expresses the crucial Disraelian insight that the social imagination, at its most concrete and powerful, is Tory. And of course the actual examples of reform here deplored—the legislative results of the post-1832 Parliaments (whether under Whigs or conservative administrations)—are Disraeli's too. Yet there's none of Disraeli's commitment to a high politics against Whiggish or utilitarian reform: the narrator merely represents a generous, sensitive, tolerant response to the life of the parish from the distance of skeptical and educated gentility.

The parish itself is inhabited by tradesmen and working people, whose most important division, both political and religious, is between Dissent and Anglicanism. Unlike Fielding's or Jane Austen's communities, for instance, it has no squire and no resident gentlemanly vicar. And the point of the story is that the Shepperton parish is *not* a community in the Burkean or Disraelian sense. It is no hierarchical organic order undergoing degradation through the implementation of reformist rationality. Rather it is a complex, mundane, conversationally democratic network that is constantly being ordered and disordered by the circulation of rumors, battles of will, clashes of personal style and tact, and eddies of emotion, mainly negative. Envy, complacency, and selfishness figure largely. The external agency of purposive ethical government in this world is not the state and certainly not the kind of state concerned with the population's secular health and education that was to form after 1832. Rather, activism from above, as represented by clergymen, applies religious doctrine and ecclesiology, especially in Sunday sermons. Yet Barton's sermons in particular are all but meaningless in the sense that they do not communicate to his parishioners. They quite fail to connect to ordinary life in the parish.

What works, at least for a moment, to transform that life into a hallowed community is Milly's death and Amos's reaction to it. This means that the fiction is organized through the tropes of a displaced Christology: it is the sacrificial death of an innocent that for a moment transforms the town's anomic conversational democracy into something like Disraelian theocratic equality.

Milly's death, and the collective emotion and the charity (in the full Christian sense) that it elicits, displace the hierarchy of idiolects and intelligence. Indeed, it moves us as readers and therefore helps culturally to democratize us too.

The story's argument—that sympathy and sacrifice trump discourse, doctrine, and sermonizing—requires that a picture rather than a diagram of Shepperton be given. Only through dense, close-to-the-ground realism, attentive to the everyday, can the parish's life be represented as simultaneously demotic and impervious to Amos's churchmanship. That realism does not quite adhere to the stylistic order that will be mandated by the modern criticism as I described it in the previous chapter. But nonetheless, in its emphasis on the concrete and vivid, it is headed in that direction. It is as if the supersession of ordinary experience and the break with neighborly niggling, envy, and suspicion that Milly's death sets into play requires Eliot to write in a mode in which she can represent the textures of ordinary felt life but without succumbing to any leveling or, for that matter, nostalgic impulses. In this context, it is worth recalling that T. S. Eliot thought "Amos Barton" by the far the best of George Eliot's fictions (Eliot 1994, 207).

A moment of hard, almost political democratization punctuates Eliot's intimately observed everydayness. It, along with Milly's death, seals the plot. It happens when the Bartons' servant, Nanny (they only employ a single "maid of all work"), loses patience with their overstaying and expensive guest, the countess, and speaks her mind.[15] The countess asks Nanny:

> "What do you mean by behaving in this way?"
>
> "Mean? Why I mean as the missis is a-slavin her life out an' a-sittin up o' nights, for folks as are better able to wait of *her*, I'stid o' lyin' a-bed an' doin' nothin' al the blessed day, but mek work."
>
> "Leave the room and don't be insolent."
>
> "Insolent! I'd better be insolent than like what some folks is,—a-livin' on other folks, an' bring' a bad name on 'em into the bargain."
>
> Here Nanny flung out of the room, leaving the lady to digest this unexpected breakfast at her leisure.
>
> The countless was stunned for a few moments, but when she began to recall Nanny's works, there was no possibility of avoiding very unpleasant conclusions from them, or of failing to see her present position at the vicarage in an entirely new light. The interpretation too of Nanny's allusion to a "bad name" did not lie out of the reach of the Countess's imagination, and she saw the necessity of quitting Shepperton without delay. (Eliot 1900, 61)

This is a rare moment in English fiction: a servant, and a very humble servant at that, speaks the truth to a countess in a situation where they have rough conversational equality across class idiolects and in such a way as actively to right an injustice and improve other lives. The narrator, for all his intimacy with the characters and their world, here gives way for a plebeian voice, at some remove from received English, to find an instrumental and direct power not available to any of the educated, genteel characters. It's a performance or, better, a realization of equality. But not, of course, in a mode that is prophetic or even supportive of formal political democracy-as-equality. Indeed, the implication would seem to be rather that a form of everyday-life theocratic equality, which is not grounded in formal moral, social, or religious principles, can be supported just because ordinary life contains spontaneous and profound democratic moments such as this one. And it can be supported even though—or perhaps, because—that ordinary life, when concretely pictured, shows itself *not* to be democratic through and through.

So at least at this point of George Eliot's career, this conversation represents where democracy mainly happens and should happen. Milly must die, and moral sensibility and charity must triumph over conversational democracy, because such insubordinate conversations, while immensely valuable, are rare, and to extend them into society and politics more generally would, from the narrator's point of view, threaten ordered sociability and institutions. And the test of sensibility and charity is how they work in an everyday—an experienced—world that literature joins by using formal and rhetorical techniques quite unlike Disraeli's, for instance. From Eliot's perspective, a literature that is close to experience itself (to invoke, admittedly, a term that neither Disraeli nor Eliot use in this context) remits demands for political democracy not because it *represents* moments of charity and brief communal spiritual awakening like those that follow Milly's death but because it can cause them. If Disraeli's novels were aimed at presenting a civic imaginary to which practical conservative politics could attach to as the franchise was extended, and do so more or less in defiance of life as experienced, then Eliot is concerned to offer illusions of a thick social world in terms that will reduce the sway of the political as the state knows the political.

It would, of course, be possible to choose other texts than Tocqueville's, Disraeli's, and George Eliot's to illuminate the relation between literature and democracy at the moment when the political triumph of democracy first became predictable. Whitman, Hawthorne, Charlotte Brontë, and Dickens are immediately obvious candidates. But I doubt even choosing these authors would markedly weaken the claim that I am making: that the democracy and democratic idea is then influentially imagined—and shaped—by its adversaries. In particular, Tocqueville's careful accounting of the costs and benefits of American democracy, along with his immunity to democratic enthusiasm, possess a vivid concreteness that, on the one side, undercuts the appeal of mystical democracy as articulated by Melville in *Moby Dick* and, on the other, resonates with the political implications of even Hawthorne's, Brontë's, and Dickens's forms of realism. We can recall that Whitman himself came to set real, fraternal, and spiritual democracy *against* the democracy that had developed during his lifetime in America (Whitman 1982, 930). But what is more remarkable still about Tocqueville is the way in which his highly developed sense of the danger that democracy poses for both social cohesion and cultural achievement is matched by his tolerance for conversational, and even a certain cultural, democracy—his appreciation, in short, of American manners and styles of life. That tolerance is something he shares with Disraeli and Eliot as they, in their very different ways, insert conservative content into the gap that political and social democratization installs between the substance and the procedures of collective life. It is their literary sensitivity to the interplay between different modalities of democratization, along with their suspicion of the terms on which democratic modernity was being promoted, that makes them important figures in the history of our current condition.

SIX

Howards End's Socialism

E. M. Forster's 1910 novel *Howards End* records the descent of the "angel of democracy" on Britain. In testifying to this annunciation, Forster was not just registering the social democratic state's emergence but engaging the ways in which everyday life was being reshaped by democratizing forces and hopes. And against a critical consensus that has invested a great deal in Forster's liberalism, I want here to argue that *Howards End*, as a political novel, adjudicates the democratic angel's contested purposes and effects inside a lineage that is closer to radicalism than to liberalism but that is already, only twenty-five years after working-class men had won the vote in Britain, more than skeptical about actual democratic possibilities.[1]

To make this case, some historical context and definition is required. Let's say that a social democracy comes into being when a government is chosen through the machinery of representative democracy, when the central state actively sets economic policy and commands significant sections of the means of production, and when social policy is oriented toward ensuring every citizen's capacity to flourish by securing basic standards of living and social security for all. In Britain, a version of social democracy, thought like this, began to emerge in the early nineteenth century (with philosophical reformers like Edwin Chadwick's centralizing policies), but its groundwork was really established in the first decade of the twentieth century. It is true, as Marxian historians in particular have argued, that the early social democratic state's main tendency was to implement policies associated with Chartism and socialism as saving supplements to capitalism, so that social democracy can be regarded as big business and finance capital's mainly reluctant accommodation to organized labor.[2] But there was also a steady, if by no means uniform, demand for social democracy from below, from the enfranchised working class and others, to allow them to participate fully in public and working life. Certainly, the propertied classes experienced the shift into social democracy more as a dangerous social fragmentation than as a progressive expansion of institutions and potentials.[3]

Britain's shift into this mode of social democracy was driven by proximate forces whose relative impact historians still dispute. These included the trade unions taking charge of working-class politicization; the decline of the established Church's social authority; the shock to imperialist patriotism occasioned in particular by the Boer Wars during the period of hyperimperialism between about 1880 and 1910; the threat to traditional patriarchy by women's will to full social participation; the splitting of both major parties over colonial issues (the Liberals by Irish Home Rule and the Tories by Joseph Chamberlain's Tariff Reform, which would have built a tariff wall around the empire); and the coming to power of a professional, policy-oriented bureaucracy (as represented by figures such as Halford Mackinder and Sidney and Beatrice Webb), whose authority was secured by its connection to social science as well as by its dual focus on national security and so-called pauperism. Most of all, entry into social democracy was driven by the decline of British productivity relative to Germany and the United States. Thus, for instance, David Lloyd George's National Insurance Act (1911), which imitated Bismarckian legislation, was aimed at socializing the costs of capitalist production in the interests of national efficiency as much as at ameliorating poverty in the interests of social justice.

The appropriation of radical policies by proponents of liberal capitalism, first under the name "new liberalism" and then as social democracy proper, refigured citizenship itself. Citizenship was now available within a contract in which the state took over management and control of civil society in exchange for establishing generalized (if rather indirect) political participation along with the universal provision of basic life amenities as some protection against the uncertainties and inequities that no market-based society can avoid.

The state's management of civil society involved some sacrificial victims: most notably, men with a taste for the sodomy that Henry Labouchere's contribution to the Criminal Law Amendment Act of 1885 criminalized, but also strangers like the immigrant Jews and Chinese who were increasingly demonized and refused acceptance into the national social democratic contract. It also reoriented social hierarchies, opening out spaces for a certain conversational democracy: it reduced the deference due to those who inherited gentility (that is, "ladies" and "gentlemen") and promoted rank divisions based on the acquisition of both capital and education.

My purpose in outlining this history in some detail is to show that the emergence of social democracy can be regarded as a dilution of that (Rousseauian) democratic and philosophic enthusiasm that we have seen articulated by Herman Melville, for instance. But such enthusiasm did not entirely disappear during the period of British social democraticization. On the contrary. It was channeled into small associations that were developed as post-Christian, so-called new-life movements. The Theosophical Society, the Shelley Society, the Browning Society, the Vegetarian Society, the Ethical Society, the Society for Psychical Research, the early women's emancipation movement (including Karl Pearson's Men and Women's Club), the Humanitarian League, and the Hermetic Society were all established around 1880.[4] The degree to which such groups eroded barriers between the political, the economic, the philosophical, the scientific, the literary, and the ethicospiritual is a sign of how intense the moment's dangers and expectations were. Famously, for instance, the Fabian Society, which was in fact to staff social democracy's state bureaucracy and whose authority was secured by its hardheaded connection to imperialism and the social sciences, emerged out of the "New Fellowship" group of radical democrats to which theosophists including Annie Besant and ethical revolutionaries such as Edward Carpenter also belonged.

The primary concept that allowed such associations to proliferate was *collectivism*. We can put it like this: social democracy was based on an antiliberal concept of society as an integrated, autotelic domain that secured not just the rights and safety of individuals but the conditions in which they could develop and prosper. Such a concept was required to replace both tradition and private property rights by social improvement and justice as primary policy values. In the process, however, society became entangled with older notions of community as well as with concepts like the theosophist's "world soul."

To complicate matters further, the coming of social democracy reordered historical temporality. As Marcel Gauchet has recently argued, after the 1880s the present thickened in comparison to the past: it is no accident that the democratic moment knew itself precisely as "modern" (Gauchet 2007, 118–128). It was not just that the present was perceived as unmoored from the past and that transgenerational flows therefore became more problematic. The future also became more contingent. This is apparent, for instance, in George Sorel's *Reflections on Violence* (1906), where myth is embraced as a ground for political resistance exactly because the future is considered thoroughly unpredictable (Sorel 1999, 116). As we will see, it is in these terms that certainty is also devalued and risk and prophecy embraced in *Howards End*.

From a literary-historical perspective, however, it is remarkable that first-wave democratic modern writing was largely authored by men and women removed from the forces that were shaping social democracy in Britain and who had, instead, experienced social exclusion, either as queer or as settler-colonials, or as both. Let me draw attention to three such writers who can especially help us fix *Howards End*'s setting and ends.

Olive Schreiner

The first is Olive Schreiner, whose *The Story of an African Farm* appeared in 1883. Schreiner, who immigrated to London from South Africa, made her metropolitan career at the intersection between socialist politics, sex and gender activism, and the social sciences, becoming active in London's new-life associations. Her novel is set in South Africa's arid Karoo, which is regarded as so isolated, so depopulated, so without hierarchies and institutions that society is barely constituted there at all. Hence the forms of the realist novel fall apart: third-person omniscience devolves into unpredictable shifts of tone and genre, characters are not recognizable types, their interiorities are opaque to themselves and others, and their stories do not proceed through received mechanisms of recognition and resolution. By the same stroke, favored characters die young and unfulfilled, victims of accident and injustice. Nonetheless, in the Karoo, everyone is equally culturally endowed, potentially at least. Its zero-degree society constitutes a primitive cultural democracy for which the novel displays no nostalgia but that does produce two good people: the orphan Lyndall, who is granted dignity because her drive to truth is unsullied by conventionality, and the farm laborer Waldo, who breaks free from Christianity and respectability to find personal practical decency within existential breakdown.

The Story of an African Farm's astonishing sales signaled not just rifts in late-Victorian respectability but an expansion of cultural participation: its commercial success expresses a metropolitan desire for a colonial desocializing imagination upon which to base a more equal society. So the challenge that the novel poses is this: How can we build a society that, on the one side, can nourish the personal integrity and autonomy that Lyndall and Waldo possess but that also meets the longing for order, justice, and cultural accomplishment that flows simultaneously from the colonies to the center and from the present to the future? The answer is that such a society will draw on the innocent, fragile, comradely love and intimacy that exists between Lyndall and Waldo and whose grounds are, paradoxically, their vulnerability to chance, exclusion, and cruelty.

Edward Carpenter

The second of the literary events underpinning the emergence of the democratic modern has no settler-colonial context, although it too is not just British. I'm referring to the publication of the various editions of Edward Carpenter's *Towards Democracy* between 1883 and 1905.[5] *Towards Democracy* collected a series of poems and prose poems influenced by Whitman's politics and poetics as well as sharing Whitman's love of men. It was written out of secularized Christian socialism: before losing his faith, Carpenter had been F. D. Maurice's curate, and the queer, communal market garden he established at Millthorpe retains certain connections to hallowed Anglican parochial communities—Nicholas Ferrar's Little Gidding, for instance. Carpenter was also committed to an irreligious Shelleyan romanticism that posited the interdependence of truth, poetry, goodness, sexuality, beauty, and freedom (and which the Shelley Society then disseminated). It drew, further, on Eastern mysticism. This enabled Carpenter to posit a universal self or "cosmic consciousness," whose energies would "inevitably revolutionize all our views of Morality—since current morality is founded on the separation of self from self" (Carpenter 1916, 207).

From one side, Carpenter's mystical democracy was a poetic orientation toward a joyous eschatological event in which democratic liberty, based on society's trumping of the individual and a return to nature, peace, and transparency, would unleash an imaginative force shared by all. We have already encountered an intimation of this spiritual and poetic politics in the passage from *Moby Dick* cited in Chapter 5, but, from Whitman after the Civil War on, mystical democracy changes complexion because it becomes directed against, and imagined as an alternative to, liberal political democracy—the democracy of the franchise, and hence "the people's crudeness, vice, caprices," in Whitman's Tocquevillean words (Whitman 1982, 930; for context, see Loving 1999, 320ff.).

From the other side, Carpenter's mystical democracy insisted that acts of sexual love, especially across classes and between men, might create eddies of democratic affect and will and nurture new forms of community. "Lust idealizes," as Forster wrote in his notebook around the time that he was writing *Howards End* (Forster 1998, 274). While in its most radical forms, mystical democracy's appeal was limited, it nonetheless flowed into socialist and new liberal politics more generally. To cite one of many cases, even the rationalist Liberal theorist L. T. Hobhouse claimed (in 1911) that the liberal project was aimed at "the liberation of living spiritual energy" (Hobhouse 1911, 137).[6]

Samuel Butler

The next of my modernizing and democratizing literary events was Samuel Butler's fictional autobiography, *The Way of All Flesh* (1903). It reveals a very different side of the modern moment: Butler was an esoteric Tory who believed that, to maintain social order, most other people needed to believe much more than he himself could. He certainly lacked sympathy for democracy in its political, mystical, and cultural forms. Like Carpenter and Schreiner, however, he was an enemy of received hierarchies and values and, at the level of everyday sociability and experience, an egalitarian. At any rate, he was a conversational democrat. And he was an exceptionally influential apostle of the modern moment, with the generation that came to maturity after Butler's death insisting on his shaping influence on them.[7] When Virginia Woolf, for instance, famously claimed that in 1910 human nature changed, an event that she cites as triggering that change was none other than the (posthumous) publication of Butler's novel.[8]

Butler's commitment to the modern was also grounded in his colonial experiences. He came from an affluent Anglican clergy family, but his inability to join a profession and his lack of interest in marriage (he fell in love with gay men, although he routinely had sex with women) led him to join a colonial settlement proper to an Anglican gentleman, namely the Wakefieldian Canterbury Association established in 1849 to settle large tracts of New Zealand's South Island.

Instead of the traditional rural community as counterrevolutionary Tories imagined it and as Edward Gibbon Wakefield had projected for his colonial settlements, Butler encountered a world, not wholly unlike Schreiner's Karoo, that fractured his relations to British society.[9] His experience is traced in *A First Year in the Canterbury Settlement* (1863), in which an English gentleman turns pretty much for the first time in print unaffectedly to the manual labor required of the pioneering colonial farmer.[10] Butler sheared, fenced, scabbed sheep, built and lived in a mud-floor hut; he walked across mountains where no European had gone before. He mixed with people from a range of backgrounds and races with the easy New Zealand masculine sociability that would come to be called mateship. In sum, for Butler the Canterbury experience meant liberation from what he described as the "science-ridden, culture-ridden, afternoon-tea-ridden cliffs of Old England" across various registers of his life (Butler 1914, 304).

At the level of life-practice, Canterbury meant a line of flight into self-sufficiency, into physical work and pragmatism. It allowed Butler to remark, in an apothegm whose full radical force is hard to recover: "To love god is to have good health, good looks, good sense, experience, a kindly nature and fair balance of cash in hand" (Cole 1948, 40). It also allowed him to develop a heretical Darwinism in which life attaches to what is transmitted rather than to those who consciously feel themselves alive. In a line of analysis we might label "romantic Spinozism," he recasts and radically diminishes the opposition between life and death. For Butler, people live on in the traces they leave in the world just as the past lives on in us in the memories, conscious or unconscious, that inhabit us. But the relation between conscious life and matter remains fundamentally mysterious. All matter (stones, rivers, trees, everything) possesses a degree of consciousness, and consciousness does not have any ontological grounding except in matter—even if matter does not *cause* consciousness. Given this, neither consciousness nor life can be accounted for within any rational system based on the principle of causation, nor is there any reflexive relation between the rational and the real. So Butler's metaphysics heightens the world's mystery at the same time that it immanentizes ontology and reorients the division between life and death. It's an ambitious form of the pantheism that Tocqueville predicted would come to dominate the democratic epoch.

The Way of All Flesh presents itself as Ernest Pontifex's story. Ernest—Butler's alter ego—is tyrannized by his unimaginative father, who is compensating for having been bullied by *his* father. And the two institutions that the family most serves are again savagely criticized: the Church is a nest of falsity, and the education required to inculcate gentlemanliness is a torture machine. Ernest's trajectory requires him to reject not just his father's authority but his family's emotional bonds and the values and structures that support those bonds. Very scandalously, Ernest allows his children to grow up declassed, as happy laborers, delivered over to a future liberated from gentlemanly training, ready to enact the truth-regime of Butler's own books. And at the novel's end, Ernest attains the style of life that Butler himself pioneered around his friendships with other intellectual, apolitical, parahomosexual, urban dissidents, a form of sociability adequate to romantic Spinozism, we might say. And which involved more isolated and privatized networks than the prophetic new-life associations, if no less *modern*.

E. M. Forster

I want to argue that the modern project that Schreiner, Carpenter, and Butler did so much to inaugurate, along with the competing forms of democracy that underpinned it, were channeled into literary history most successfully by E. M. Forster.[11] Two qualifications to this claim need immediately to be acknowledged, however.

First, Forster is a modern writer insofar as he negotiates tensions between Butler and Carpenter in particular. Forster was personally inspired by both men. For instance, he fictionalized aspects of both their personalities in his novels. Just after 1910, he intended to write a monograph on Butler, and it was while visiting Carpenter that he had the epiphany that led him to write *Maurice*. Less anecdotally: while Carpenter's mystical democracy retains some force in Forster's work, as we will see, Forster is also a modern in Butler's sense. Forster's take on Butler may not be quite what we might expect, though. Mainly, Butler's ontology helped shape *Howards End* in particular, in which death loses much of its sting and in which a house and a tree become mysterious spiritual agents. No less important, however, as Forster noted, it was Butler who "taught me how to look at money" positively, that is to say, reconciled Forster to life under capitalism and thus constrained his welcome of Carpenter's mystical democracy (Beauman 1993, 168).

Second, Forster follows Schreiner, Carpenter, and Butler only within the limits of another more received literary tradition—the moral realism established by writers like Jane Austen.[12] That's because Forster is not so much a writer who anticipates a fractional and committed audience as he is one who wished to communicate widely. He was committed to realism, at least in part because he was a pedagogue. We can remember that for years he taught at the Working Men's College, and after the war he was a prolific radio broadcaster. So in his novels, reaching out to a wide public, Forster carries on the modern project by presenting it in reworked versions of familiar mimetic conventions, especially (1) the use of a third-person narrative voice, if a third-person voice whose relation to the indirect free style is much less stable than even in predecessors like Henry James; (2) the presentation of characters that at least seem to typify recognizable moral and social formations and the allocation of a rich interiority only to the most sympathetic of them; and (3) the fusing of narrative closure with (at least some kind of) moral or ethicopolitical resolution. None of these devices were as confidently deployed by Schreiner or Butler or by the "modernists" proper.

HOWARDS END

Howards End is a novel about two families, the Schlegels and the Wilcoxes, and a house—Howards End.

Henry Wilcox is a businessman making a fortune in imperial trade and who has "bought forests from the natives for a few bottles of gin" (Forster 1998, 201). His family enjoys the leisure activities of the uncultivated rich: golf, conspicuous consumption, motoring. They are attached to the Victorian chivalric code and the cult of "character"; they adhere to conventional class and gender prejudices. And they reject the state's management of civil society: Mr. Wilcox dismisses Parliament as a talking shop and flatly declares, "there is no Social Question" (138). In them, Gladstonian liberalism, whose moral basis had been undermined by imperialism and the concentration of finance capital, has become selfish and conservative, and it's easy to see why commentators today can regard them as previsions of late twentieth-century neoliberalism (Beauman 1993, 221; Mulhern 2000, 35). Yet in their lack of interest in high-cultural distinction and their frank acceptance of money's power, they too are modern, at least in Butler's sense. Indeed, Mr. Wilcox is a cultural democrat in a very different way than Schreiner's characters: he believes that each class has its own integral corporate culture within which individuals should remain. His liberal views (whose principles at least are familiar to us in contemporary celebrations of *difference*) can be accepted neither by those who live in poverty but aspire to high-cultural experiences nor by bourgeois social democrats like the Schlegel sisters who expect that substantive social egalitarianism would be accompanied by universal cultural elevation.

One of the Wilcoxes' properties is Howards End, which had been inherited by Henry's wife and in which she was born. Although still connected to agrarianism, it is not now, and never was, a landed estate (it was owned by Quakers) and bears no traces of feudal or Austenian class hierarchy. Apart from Mrs. Wilcox, the family does not appreciate the house: it is becoming part of a London suburb—it's at risk by modernizing processes—and anyway they consider it "impossibly small" (Forster 1998, 99). But unlike their other houses, it contains a unique ethos, which Mrs. Wilcox, her housekeeper Mrs. Avery, and her friend Margaret Schlegel all come to share. That ethos is embodied (in a Butlerian fashion) in a wych elm, which is not just a vehicle for old folk traditions but also a quasi-socialist "comrade" (148). After her death, Mrs. Wilcox's memory presides over the house—"She knows everything. She *is* everything," as Margaret says. She becomes a shamanistic presence in the house, preternaturally ordering life from beyond the grave. At the novel's end, Margaret and Helen Schlegel take command of Howards End in turn, preserving their predecessor's ethos into the era of social democracy and imperialism, in what is in effect a feminist microcosm of both Schreiner's cultural and Carpenter's mystical democracy.

The Schlegel sisters, Margaret and Helen, and their brother, Tibby, are parentless. In their twenties, they have inherited sufficient capital to live the cultivated life in London without working. They are half German, and their Germanness survives in their passion for culture and ideas, their socialism, and their sense of the "invisible" and (in Helen's case) the absolute, which sometimes takes the form of a curiosity about new-life movements, including theosophy. It is from these transcendental sources that the Schlegels' commitment to political justice is bound to their love of high culture. Margaret is a socialist because, in a Butlerian sense, she recognizes that "the very soul of the world is economic" (165). She stands, in Forster's shorthand, for the "true." But Helen tends toward socialism because of her passion for social justice, a passion also expressed in her secular understanding of death and appreciation of beauty.[13] She stands, in short, for "love." She is, indeed, aligned with Carpenterian mystical democracy, as becomes clear when she has sex with a young uneducated London clerk, Leonard Bast, despite her sense that he is not her equal, and then when, after Bast's death, imitating Schreiner's Lyndall, she gives birth to their illegitimate child despite being socially ostracized as a consequence. That child will be brought up at Howards End, like Butler's Ernest Pontifex's children, declassed.

The story told in *Howards End* heads in two directions. On one side, both Schlegel sisters have love relations with Wilcox men. Helen experiences a gust of sexual passion for the Wilcoxes' youngest son, Paul, just before he leaves for the colonies in part because he represents a mode of masculine "character" and physicality that is unavailable in her own circles. Margaret has a more serious relationship: she marries Mr. Wilcox after his wife's death. Margaret's love for Henry is possible because she does not share her siblings' scorn for the Wilcox ethos. She too is suspicious of organized efforts to convert the badly educated to bourgeois high culture (she believes that, at least until socialism is realized, economic and cultural inequality should be addressed not by governmental cultural or hygienic intervention but simply by distributing capital more generally to the poor). And she recognizes not just that cultivated, progressive intellectuals like herself are in fact dependent on a world built by hardheaded, unscrupulous, "obtuse" businessmen like Henry Wilcox but also that Henry's unembarrassed, not quite gentlemanly commitment to practical and imperial moneymaking is an unavoidable aspect of English democratic modernity more generally.

On the other side, the Schlegels accidentally meet Leonard Bast. He belongs to the salaried petit-bourgeoisie, working for that peculiarly modern organization—the large corporation—and so is marked off from the educated and the entrepreneurial upper middle classes (that is, from the Wilcoxes and Schlegels) as well as from the nonsalaried working class. He is an uneducated, aspiring reader of Ruskin, Thoreau, George Borrow, and so on—who figure for him, I'd suggest, as popularizations of the mystical-democracy lineage. These aspirations mark him out from George Eliot's townspeople in "Amos Barton," who resist, or are indifferent to, or are represented as too dull to accept bourgeois *garantiste* pedagogy. They also mark him out from characters like George Gissing's Richard Mutimer in *Demos* (1880), who have connections to political laborism and Marxism and who therefore are compromised by their aspirations to gentility. And most of all, they mark him out from the working-class characters in D. H. Lawrence's *Sons and Lovers* (1913), in which, for the first time, the English literary novel presents proletarian life without a trace of bourgeois condescension, knowing that relatively secure and rational (if restricted) institutional channels for joining the educated middle classes, outside of patronage connections, are in place.

Bast lacks the resources to live out the values and experiences that are celebrated in the books that he reads. So, for instance, his attempt to embark on an adventurous night on the road à la Stevenson and Borrow ends in bathos. Worse than that, the conditions of his life, which he inherits rather than chooses, of course, fail to offer him opportunities for true love. And this failure, in particular, sanctions the novel's own social democratic straining toward a polity in which restrictions and suffering such as he knows will no longer be tolerated, a straining that is felt among the novel's characters most intensely by Helen Schlegel.

Near the end of the novel, Bast is killed by Henry Wilcox's son, Charles, for supposedly seducing Helen—in a Butleresque reduction of the gentlemanly honor code into sheer, stupid brutality. That causes Margaret, Henry Wilcox, Mrs. Avery, Helen, and her baby boy to set up house at Howards End and establish an alternative, new-life community there. Howards End is a version of Carpenter's queer-democratic Millthorpe—a place where the past is channeled into the present by spiritual forces so to protect a form of democratic communitarianism based on love. Or to take a different line of entry, it is a fragile Schreinerian colonial outpost within the metropolis (and hence rooted in a placed English past) where personal relations reign supreme. In sheltering Henry Wilcox and Leonard Bast's son as well as the Schlegel sisters and Mrs. Avery, this community combines the cultural and mystical strands of the modern democratic moment. Yet it is one of the novel's deepest ironies that Bast's failed relation to high culture and the liberation it encourages is in the end shared by the Schlegels themselves, since Forster shows that the complex commitment to democracy that Howards End represents cannot be successfully lived out except in the relative isolation in which love takes its distance from truth.

Howards End is, as I say, a pedagogic text. It often uses the simplifying tone of instruction, but in the end, its educational vector is handled through a remarkable formal innovation.[14] Forster combines a pedagogic technique of repeating simple ethical apothegms or laws with a Wagnerian technique of aestheticizing phrasal repetition, what he called "patterning."[15] The novel's pedagogic phrases are often also structuring leitmotifs, and as such they partly replace a conventional narrative conspectus, which is already undermined by the degree to which it is impossible to decide whether important sentences belong to a character or to the narrator.

The novel's most famous such law is "only connect." It's a phrase that points in various directions, the most obvious being toward the concept of social totality. To connect is to see, for instance, that Bast's poverty is the necessary condition for the wealth of the Wilcoxes and Schlegels and that Henry Wilcox's long-ago affair with Bast's wife, Jackie, is not to be distinguished morally from Helen's encounter with Bast. At any rate, connecting prevents individuals from falling into classical liberalism. It also prevents them either from obtusely taking full responsibility for their actions and personalities or from fetishizing individuality itself and thus from masking the creative power that belongs only to social being or consciousness. "Connect without bitterness until all men are brothers," Margaret says to herself at Howards End, gesturing to the fraternal ideal, as Butlerian truth begins to fail her.

The opposite of connection is "muddle," which here is seen as the existential condition that has the most power on those who, like the Wilcoxes and Basts, are most under liberal capitalism's control and thus tend to fall into what in another leitmotif is named "panic and emptiness" and which, as a result, is also linked to the failure of cultural democracy and to the cynical belief that "there is no such thing as splendor and heroism in the world" (Forster 1998, 26). Muddle often happens in the undemocratic and irrational play of will and desire in everyday life. It is immersed in experience or, better, in experience's flailing about for exceptional significance. The infinity that London expresses in the novel—a Hegelian "bad infinity"—is also a muddle that is endless in the sense that it can't be ordered by connections. A muddled life also compromises relations to what exists at the very limits of connectivity; that is, it blocks passages to Forster's "invisible." The invisible is a secular concept here, even if, like Butler's mystery, it names all that secular experience and reason cannot grasp. The invisible's home in the novel is Howards End itself, and its primary characterological vehicle is the first Mrs. Wilcox, with her intuitive and prophetic powers, her "aristocratic" connection to the past (18), and her capacity to live near "the line that divides daily life from a life that may be of greater importance" (58).

It is in relation to muddle on the one side and the invisible on the other that "only connect" moves past the Arnoldian concept of culture ("seeing things whole" and seeing things "as they are") to which it seems close, since in relation to the invisible, connecting cannot be called upon simply to do the work of cultivation. "Culture is not an end," as Forster puts it in the novel (183). And so, equally, it is by virtue of the invisible that culture can be imagined as mystically democratic and not merely as conversationally or socially democratic. Connected to Carpenter's democratic love and fraternalism, the invisible operates like a Christian grace that mysteriously exceeds totality and institutional affiliation. Indeed, a democratic deadlock between love and truth becomes visible just because the invisible cannot be encountered via institutions such as those that belong to the state. It is Margaret's exceptional power to understand this that marks her out (24). So there can be no easy passage from mystical to social democracy. That's why, at the novel's end, Howards End's little community transcends capitalist social democracy and resists the leveling and emptying power of populist cultural egalitarianism by virtue of its *disconnection* from society. Yet it is not as if we can be confident that either mystical democracy or an elevated cultural democracy are to be realized more widely in the future.

In sum, these quite complex relations between (1) connection, which is finally the domain of order and social democracy; (2) muddle, the domain of capitalism's sites of stupidity and ignorance; and (3) the invisible or secular ontological mystery provides much of the energy for a force field that the novel sets in play and that allows it to fictionalize a complex commitment to democracy, with its multifariousness, tensions, and incapacities when it encounters the experienced world—all this within a residually pedagogic, realist narratological form.

But, by Forster's own critical theory, the novel reveals its mystical democratic straining only via a particular hermeneutic technique, one that can distinguish its good from its bad readers. In *Aspects of the Novel* (1927), Forster proposed that novels can be organized through structures that belong neither to genre nor to form nor to characterology nor to figurative patterns. These he named "fantasy" and "prophecy." Fantasy textually enacts the unaccountable and irrational play of and between events at the level of mundane everydayness: his chief example is the all but supernatural "muddle" that *Tristram Shandy* brings to life. Prophecy enacts relations to the transcendental in prose-fictional song: one of Forster's examples is the way in which, in *Moby Dick*, the narrative role of Queequeg's coffin cannot be accounted for rationally or critically, and in the end any effort to turn it into a symbol "only silences the book," which Forster understands as lyricizing cosmic "contest" (Forster 1962b, 144). The prophetic is only revealed when contingency and literalness are allowed their full force, since only then can the work "reach back" into the constitution of the world. So at the point at which literature becomes most profound, the reader is not to *interpret* the text but to stay with the present-to-hand. In critiquing the will to interpret Forster joins, from the other side, modern literary criticism as described above as well as antidemocratic modernists like T. E. Hulme and Leo Strauss, for whom literary interpretation was connected to destabilizing, self-glorifying Protestantism, liberalism, and romanticism.

We need antihermeneutic tact to read *Howards End* properly. Take its final sentences. Helen Schlegel, at Howards End, is talking to Margaret and Henry. She is holding her baby in her arms and Tom, a farm laborer's son, by the hand. She shouts to Henry Wilcox:

> "The field's cut!" Helen cried excitedly—"the big meadow! We've seen to the very end, and it'll be such a crop of hay as never!"

It's a passage that may be interpreted figuratively either as anticipating a more productive and harmonious future or, given Helen's unstandard syntax, as the opposite—there'll never be a crop of hay this large again, an ambiguity that reveals how uncertain the future is. It is true that throughout the novel Forster invokes natural things—in particular, flowers and the sea and its estuaries—as figures for psychological or social forms. And it is especially tempting to read this passage figuratively, because the transmutation of grass to hay (through withering to sweetness) has been described by Helen in terms that signal a progressive understanding of history, while the hay's heterogeneity—it consists of sorrel; red, white, and yellow clover; quaker grass; daisies; and bents—signals the "difference" for which Margaret "battles against sameness" (Forster 1998, 239). And, of course, we first met Mrs. Wilcox with hay in her hand, and she is later named, in a metaphor, a "wisp of hay" herself (56): a "wisp of hay" that later in the novel becomes a metaphor simply for "death" (234). Last, we also know that the Wilcox family's propensity to hay fever has helped keep them from fully appreciating Howards End, so their allergy can also signify their insensitivity to the house's memory channels and mystical community. But for the novel to work prophetically in Forster's terms, such readings must be resisted.

The big meadow is a big meadow, the hay crop is a hay crop, hay fever is hay fever, and the accident by which some people suffer from the allergy and others do not is just an accident: consequential but not meaningful. What is represented here is, as it were, an experience that is prophetic because it has not yet become entangled in muddle, in signification.

Such resistance to interpretation is aligned to a certain democratic will, since only in a bare reading for which, as Paul de Man once remarked, "the literal meaning is not simpler than figurative meaning" (de Man 1979, 9) can the novel make its mystical political turn and invoke the unknowable plays of force, the impenetrable mysteries of democratic futurity, into which we must reach if the text is, as Forster puts it, to "imply" "the development of humanity" in terms other than the official liberal-left progressivism that is ultimately destructive (Forster 1998, 173). It is, of course, perfectly possible to read the novel as "tragic" in Forster's sense, a tragedy that, at the level of politics, presents a fundamental tension between mystical democracy and political democracy. (That's a version of Lionel Trilling's belief that Forster is more than a liberal because he does possess the tragic sense.) But I would prefer to go in other directions.

At the level of history, it is only if we resist the temptation to read *Howards End* as a figure for English rural life as such that it can break from its moral realism's full conservative implications, even though, admittedly, it is impossible *not* to read the community of the novel's final pages as outside conservative lineages.

At the level of plot, it is only if the hay is just hay that Helen's baby and Tom the farm boy may break from the patterns of experience and meaning (and the difficult politics of cultural democracy) that have helped divide the Schlegels, the Basts, and the Wilcoxes from one another and so to prevent them becoming, in the future, more like Schreiner's and Butler's characters than like Forster's.

At the level of political metaphysics, it is only through a spiritual humility, an acceptance of the full force of accident's power in the world, expressed in plain and literal language, that society can be disassembled and mundane life be affirmed so that an imaginative democratic project may be realized against what Helen calls "the melting down of life all over the world" (355) and in defiance of what is already emptied social hope. That process begins in the barely associational community that is Howards End, where the hopes of mystical democracy are preserved in and against a society slowly (and often, as here, reluctantly) becoming a social democracy, as I say. And, of course, the novel's readers are vehicles of that hope in the real world, especially where they resist the liberal will to interpret and the temptation to abandon democracy's fullest promise—that of a romantic Spinozan, creative spiritual awakening—by adverting to mere liberal pluralism.

But of course, given the weight of figuration upon it, in the end it is impossible to read Forster's dialogue literally. That is especially so inside academic literary studies, which now draws so much of its institutional life from interpretation. I realize that I myself am giving these sentences political and cultural significance in the gesture of denying them interpretative potential. What this means is that the question of how we do or don't interpret *Howards End* does need to be thought of not just in terms of the tensions between political (or social), mystical, and cultural democracy—not just in the terms I have been sketching—but in terms of a sustained *forgetting* of, in particular, the mystical democratic project during, first, the social democratic and, then, the neoliberal state's coming to power. One might even say that it is as if compulsory democracy has smothered mystical democracy of the kind that is still—just—alive in *Howards End* and that that smothering is, however faintly, expressed in our compulsion to interpret rather than to experience the novel.

SEVEN

Saul Bellow and the Antinomies of Democratic Experience

To the academic literary critic, few writers offer greater challenges—and, I think, greater rewards—than Saul Bellow. That's partly because he was *one of us*. For much of his career, he was a professor at the University of Chicago's Committee on Social Thought, where he taught for more than thirty years. And his novels are—whatever else they are—novels of pedagogical intent, exploring the contemporary fate of the ideas that constituted a humanities education at the time. Many of his protagonists are intellectuals—the most famous of them all, Moses Herzog, is a professor of intellectual history and the author of the academic monograph *Romanticism and Christianity*. Tellingly, at the time during which the story is set, Herzog is working on a version of our own topic, a "history which really took into account the revolutions and mass convulsions of the twentieth century, accepting, with de Tocqueville, the universal and durable development of the equality of conditions, the progress of democracy" (Bellow 2007a, 422).[1]

For all that, Bellow is something of a persona non grata in the academy today. The reasons for his lack of visibility are complex, but in summary we can say that it's because in the late 1960s he became not just a critic but an enemy—and a contemptuous enemy—of the emancipation movements by which democracy was extended into new social groups and life-world zones. Around that time, Bellow set himself against postcolonialism too: in the mid-1970s, his pro-Zionist report on his trip to Israel was received with scorn by the left, for instance (see Chomsky 1977). He also resisted feminism: the depiction of women in his novels was denounced as seconding them to male wills and desires (unfairly in the case of *The Adventures of Augie March*). And he succumbed to post–civil rights white panic. The at least apparently racist scene in his 1969 novel, *Mr. Sammler's Planet*, in which an imposing black pickpocket intimidates the novel's elderly Jewish protagonist, Mr. Sammler, by silently unzipping his fly and exposing his large penis in the lobby of an apartment building, is often cited as causing Bellow's liberal readership to turn from him.

We can, however, begin to take a more welcoming conspectus on Bellow's work and its context by suggesting that, if the emergence of social democracy was the key event in Britain while E. M. Forster was writing his novels, then the fundamentalizing of democracy, and especially the radical extension of cultural democracy, was of roughly equivalent importance during Bellow's career. At the height of the Cold War—from the late 1940s to the early 1960s—the idea of democracy was hystericized in the United States, as its affirmation became an expression and index of the United States' putatively threatened global dominance. But at the same time, American democracy was reorganizing cultural forms and relations in ways that risked established American order. It was becoming total. At least that's how it seemed to Tocqueville's conservative academic heirs, many housed in increasingly well-funded humanities faculties, of whom Daniel Bell—a friend and colleague of Bellow's—stands out.

In two important books, *The End of Ideology* (1960) and the post-1968 *Cultural Contradictions of Capitalism* (1976), Bell argued, in effect, that the marginalizing of conviction politics, along with cultural democratization, was threatening the original American democratic project, dedicated to change in the interests of a fair, tolerant, high-minded civilization (Bell 2001, 404). In *Cultural Contradictions*, indeed, American cultural democracy, driven by market forces, was jeopardizing not just American political democracy but the American ethos and experience itself. And Bell parsed this in terms he inherited from the young T. S. Eliot's literary criticism:

> The extension of vulgarity has threatened to overwhelm the serious culture; the growth of highly vocal sub-cultures has offered modes of self-absorption to significant segments of the society (*vide* the youth culture of recent years).
>
> But the underlying problem, I submit, is less these overt sociological developments than a breakup in the very discourses—the languages, and the ability of the languages to express an experience—which give culture its present incoherence. Much of this is due to the ambiguity of the term "modernity" and what it expresses. More is due to breakup of underlying syntactical structures of cultural styles. (Bell 1979, 86)

It is hard to distinguish proximate from deep causes in this analysis. But it seems as if "modernity" (which is more or less the equivalent of "democratic capitalism," at least along one axis) finally leads to cultural democratization ("vulgarity," the proliferation of subcultures). Cultural democratization, in turn, immanentizes (as it did, of course, for Tocqueville) and thereby both prevents language from cleanly articulating experience and fails to maintain "transcendental conceptions" and "litany or ritual" (86). The "incoherence" and "contradictory modes of experience" (87) that cultural democracy involves are next summed up as an "eclipse of distance" that names, severally, the dissolution of social hierarchies, the confusion of role and person, the subsumption of form and completeness by content and fragment, and the vanishing of the civilized person's distance from their own experience, including aesthetic experience. For this way of thinking, the eclipse of distance terminates in a "culture of the self *par excellence*," that is to say, in a massification of Schmitt's romantic occasionalism (132).

This tension between democracy's supreme political importance and its perceived degradation of culture and style are also key to Bellow's work. Indeed, by the 1970s he was associated with the intellectuals who were establishing the movement that was to be called "neoconservatism." Edward Shils, one of the movement's founding fathers, had recruited him to the University of Chicago. Hilton Kramer applauded his politics in *Commentary*. Bell himself used *Mr. Sammler's Planet* as evidence of the destructive demand for "a destiny that is always beyond—beyond morality, beyond tragedy, beyond culture" (Bell 1971, 44; 1979, 135–137, 168). And in 1987, Bellow encouraged his friend and colleague, the Straussian Allan Bloom, to publish the best-selling *The Closing of the American Mind*, based on a literature course that Bloom and he had co-taught. It famously (and inchoately) took issue with what it thought of as relativism, the dumbing down of standards, the contemporary cult of gratification, and so on.[2] By the 1980s, Bellow too had become dismissive of the academy itself as a system, accusing it of abandoning "the laborious task of discarding bad thought" in his preface to Bloom's book (Bellow 1987, 17). And as became particularly clear in *The Dean's December* (a novel that compares the United States to Ceausescu's Romania, not wholly to the former's advantage), Bellow's critique of the democratization of the life-world in the 1960s also became a critique of democratic state capitalism itself.

By that time, Bellow, who had been widely acknowledged as the best American novelist of his generation—one of the few whose works were essential to understanding American literature as such and who had received almost all the honors available to an American writer, including the 1976 Nobel Prize in Literature—was, as I say, losing academic critical attention.[3] Celebration of his work became confined largely to nonacademic novelists and literary journalists, many British, of whom Martin Amis, Christopher Hitchens, James Wood, Stanley Crouch, John Coetzee, and David Eggers have been particularly prominent.[4]

Yet, given the current social situation, I believe that it is time we returned more wholeheartedly to Bellow. To begin with, his reactionary response to the 1960s liberation movements, while insupportable at the time, is much less insupportable now that those movements have been absorbed into the democratic state capitalist system. These movements still retain emancipatory energy and targets, of course, but very little at the level of culture. Were the full aspirations of feminism, gay liberation, and the civil rights movement to material equality, recognition, and the eradication of prejudice to be fulfilled, the distribution and organization of experience of democratic state capitalism would still not be significantly transformed. More important, however, and as I have been arguing throughout this book, democracy's "cultural contradictions" have been reignited on a rather different terrain now that the democratic idea has no legitimate rivals.

Which is to say that, of all late twentieth-century novelists, none writes more directly than Bellow within the parameters of Tocqueville's prophecies for America. Working at the moment just prior to the appearance of compulsory democracy, when social democracy's legitimacy was beginning to fail, none is more carefully and evenly concerned with the fate of ethical and intellectual traditions and aspirations in the democratic everyday. None is more concerned with collapses and leakages of singular individuality. None is more interested in catching the feel of democratic life in what Jacques Rancière has called a "common sensorium" (Rancière 2010, 133). None is more alert to tensions between democratic experience and the democratic idea.

Yet, on the other side, for all his conservatism, Bellow is both a conversational democrat and an experiential democrat. In his novels, speech circulates independently of rank, often in defiance of verisimilitude, and, in a Tocquevillean spirit, he characteristically sets the ordinary, the stuff of everyday existence and *phronesis* against democratic state capitalism's materialism and theatricalizations. Then, too, he has immense faith in the wide distribution of intelligence: that faith fires his imaginative, fictional projections. He has no truck with Disraeli-style fictions of a ranked, organic social imaginary.

As I want to argue, in his attempt to come to terms with these tensions, Bellow became a democrat *against* the democracy in place in terms not completely dissimilar to those poststructuralist radical democrats for whom true democracy is based on a community that does not appeal to a fullness and similarity we possess by virtue of our essential human qualities. By connecting both selfhood and collective life to what exceeds the benignly human, Bellow joins a spiritual democracy of a more mystical kind than even E. M. Forster's, since it extends beyond the merely human. His is a democracy that rests on a relation to those who exist, as he himself puts it in *Mr. Sammler's Planet*, "between the human and not human states, between content and emptiness, between full and void, meaning and non-meaning, between this world and no world" (Bellow 2004, 240). His mystical democracy plays off the will to full human fellowship against humanity's cosmic provinciality.

More particularly, Bellow is democratic even though, or because, he is also a Tocquevillean liberal conservative for whom compulsory democratization is dangerous most of all because it threatens singularity, or what he calls *nobility*. This emphasis on nobility places him in a long conservative lineage, of course, but after 1968 in particular it came to have specific political resonances within that American neoconservatism to which Bellow was connected and that claimed that the "founders" had written the U.S. Constitution not simply to secure homogenous and happy communities but to allow full room for exceptional individuals to achieve greatness.[5] Bellow himself, both before and after his conservative turn, consistently explores the possibilities for, and risks of, nobility, conceived not so much as a drive to transcendence but, on the one side, as a connection to the high Western intellectual tradition and, on the other, as the testing of limits, a commitment to risk against safety and the merely human, a testing that is driven by a quasi-Platonic appetite for truth, nature, and reality at whatever cost. Except that in Bellow nobility has become "dizzy," entangled in ceaseless Forsterian muddle or, like a Schmittian romantic, in passionate immersion in and (often reluctant) assent to the contingencies of situations and occasions.

Indeed, Bellow's writing works against society as it is—he directs us toward communities of intimates bound not in Bloomsburyite friendship but in betrayal, unreason, the amoral and inhuman, even if they also may contain redemptive (if incoherent) individual flashes of nobility. If these interests thus place him close to the intellectual circles around Georges Bataille and Alexandre Kojève in Paris during the 1930s and 1940s and out of which *Inner Experience* was written (which Bellow had encountered during his time in Paris after the war and which he explicitly returned to in his later novels), it is also the case that, as for Forster, the drive to incoherent nobility as well as toward cruel intimacy becomes urgent in his work precisely because the enlightened moral and experiential bases of democracy can no longer be easily affirmed. In sum, his is a cultural politics that takes us to the place where conservatism and radical democracy meet, not least because his imagination of the noble, the inhuman, and the everyday necessarily intimates possibilities for associations, which however virtual and inavowable continue to fit Tocqueville's template for American democracy as a society that ceaselessly and creatively is required to counter passivity and uniformity.

But Bellow's posthumanist political pantheism also matters for literature, because his novels extend the formal tradition in which he was trained and that he first employed, that is, the kind of writing established for prose by Flaubert and sanctioned by the mode of literary criticism that I described in chapter 4, which we can formularize reductively enough in the phrase that R. P. Blackmur (Bellow's friend and academic patron) applied to Henry James: "what is not vivid is not represented, and what is not represented is not art" (Blackmur 1983, 18).[6] For Bellow, such writing, deploying the full armory of technique and figurative language and aiming at rescuing the "density of actual experience," could draw readers closer to a place somewhere between what life is and what life should be (Brans 1979, 68). Thought this way, Bellow's task was to bring a literary-critical norm of vital concreteness to bear upon an increasingly threatened Whitmanesque celebration of democratic openness, a norm attuned, as I have said, to disorder and the inhuman precisely because the ordered human world has failed to reconcile individual nobility to a democracy becoming both fundamental and compulsory. In so failing, democratic capitalism (Bell's "modernity") is depriving individuals of the kind of subjectivity, of the "souls," as Bellow put it in his later work, required to correct the demission of coherent and fully spiritually open social and ethical purposes.[7]

I will support this description of Bellow's project by presenting an overview of four novels that encapsulate the main phases of his career (*Dangling Man*, *The Victim*, *The Adventures of Augie March*, and *Mr. Sammler's Planet*) and then offering a somewhat fuller reading of *Herzog*, the last novel he wrote before his overtly conservative turn.

Bellow was born in 1915 into a family of recent and poor East European Jewish immigrants. He was raised in the Yiddish-speaking streets of Chicago's West Side, among refugees from Bolshevism and Russian anti-Semitism. His family felt they had come down in the world in immigrating to America. They had been displaced from an aristocratic into a democratic order, as his fictions often remind us. So although still bound to rituals of Orthodox Judaism, they encouraged the young Bellow in his interests in European high culture and thereby sealed his identification of that culture with nobility (see Bellow 2007a, 456). As was the case for Disraeli, Bellow's Jewishness seems to have attuned him to that quintessentially conservative belief that (as Irving Kristol put it), "high culture inevitably has an aristocratic bias . . . has always felt contempt for the bourgeois mode of existence" (Kristol 1971, 16).

For all that, Bellow, like many second-generation immigrants, experienced an alienating distance between his own environment and the one that had formed his parents. In his adolescence, he joined an intensely intellectual and literary Chicago circle of young Jewish men, memorably described in Steven Zipperstein's biography of Isaac Rosenfeld (Zipperstein 2009). Bellow was an active Trotskyite until 1941, when he became a Deweyian democrat, and his break with the communist left is reflected in his first novel, *Dangling Man*, which is set among the Hyde Park intellectuals of the war years. By then, Bellow had been drawn into the world and program of New York's anti-Stalinist left, and the novel can be thought of as attempting to fulfill the *Partisan Review* program for contemporary American literature, namely the fusion of European modernism with the indigenous democratic tradition, in Bellow's case especially with Theodore Dreiser's and James T. Farrell's Chicago naturalism.[8] Like Forster and like Leavis (whose work, however, he is on record as disliking), Bellow was committed to a certain realism because of his moral and political purposes.[9]

Dangling Man *(1944)*

Dangling Man is the story of a young man, known simply in modernist style as Joseph. He lives in ordinary petit-bourgeois Chicago as described in a realist mode, but he is also an everyman, an allegorical figure in the lineage of Dostoyevsky's underground man, Rilke's Malte Laurids Brigge, and Sartre's Roquentin. Joseph is idling away his time in an apartment that he shares with his wife, awaiting his military call-up, coming to terms with his own passage to becoming an American solder from being a Marxist partisan of revolution, hanging out in circles like those beautifully evoked in Alfred Kazin's (New York–based) *On Native Grounds* and *Starting Out in the Thirties*. More abstractly and in its own lexicon, *Dangling Man* tells the story of Joseph's slow and partial rejection of "alienation" along with the political and social investments attached to alienation—alienation being a concept endlessly debated among the mid-1940s left, especially the Jewish left. Alienation then had the sociological sense that Marx had given it, but it also denoted more localized disconnections, especially between Jews and Gentiles and between immigrant parents and children (see Bell 1946, Howe 1946, and Trilling 1956).[10] The concept's implications darkened during and after the war, coming to represent a dangerous Marxist-tinged dissatisfaction with an American capitalist liberal democracy that stood against fascism and communism. At the end of *Dangling Man*, and as if in anticipation of the reining in of distance and critique in the 1950s, Joseph does indeed come to accept "the supervision of the spirit" and "regimentation" that the army, as well as, implicitly, social living in the democratic state, entails (Bellow 2007b, 191). And, importantly, this submission to national discipline will allow Joseph—as a Jew—to represent an American condition tout court. From the very beginning, it had been one of Bellow's literary purposes to create Jewish characters who could represent the condition of the nation.

The overriding ethical importance of not being alienated will form one of Bellow's main messages throughout his career, and in his work the critique of alienation spills over to a critique of the power of negation as such, a critique, for instance, of Heidegger's death-centered existentialism and Kierkegaard's concept of spiritual dread. Yet for Bellow, resistance to alienation is such a dynamic and productive topic because alienation is so difficult to overcome, however determined the attempt. One reason for this difficulty is that Bellow had a sense of the immensity of America's failures that only a training in Marxism can provide. After all, he became increasingly sensitive not only to America's blindness to suffering but to its assaults on dignity, truth, and reality—often in the service of democratizing processes. It is not just that for him America punished that distinction, that will to exceptionality, which remained a supreme object of desire as well as, if more doubtfully, a legitimation of existence as such. It is also that, at the level of the personal, where social bonds are enacted and formed, no one is more alienated from his fellows than a Bellow protagonist, for whom other people, and especially those closest to him—those whom he loves—are always capable of treachery, always willing to cast others into the venal equality of petty jealousies and strivings.

So Joseph is caught in the play between affirmation and alienation. In the end, he refuses to judge society and being-in-the-world as alienating for intellectual reasons—because he believes that he is not in a position to make such a judgment. He is himself, like any naturalist character, formed by society, so he is beset by a "weakness of vision" (137). This means that his resistance to his own distance and rejection of the world is less affective than analytical and political. Alienation is for him "a feeling not a doctrine" (38). In fact, he lives under an alienation that he does not believe in or act upon, and—here's the twist— his *experience* of alienation seems intensified by his rejection of it as a principle of thought and action.

The Victim *(1947)*

Bellow's next novel, *The Victim*, marks a significant step forward, not least because Bellow comes closer to succeeding in what would become a career-long struggle with the technical question of how the narrative voice and the protagonist's voice should relate to each other. *Dangling Man* used first-person narration, but Joseph, a reflective intellectual, writes about himself as if in the third person, and indeed he often refers to himself as "Joseph." This means that *Dangling Man*'s turn to the objectifying techniques of classic realism from within first-person narration strikes another blow at its supposed overcoming of alienation, since its structure seems to express that alienation. This is not the case in *The Victim*, which is written in the third person, but a third person who characteristically hovers just over its protagonist's shoulder in impersonal intimacy—restricting itself to the character's point of view, often through extended passages of free indirect speech. The intimacy between the third-person narration and the protagonist, Abe Leventhal, allows readers to become more immersed in Leventhal's moods, meditations, memories, and associative flows than they could be through Joseph's self-objectifying first person. And since, unlike Joseph, Leventhal is not an intellectual—he's the "editor of a small trade magazine" (Bellow 2008, 1)—his experiences are more generic than Joseph's, too. Like Joseph, he lives in a crowded, polluted, close, messy, unstable urban neighborhood—this time in New York—but he's much more mobile than Joseph, so again his personal experiences spread more widely into the public world.

There's a real plot this time as well. Leventhal is accosted by Allbee, an old acquaintance who, to Leventhal's initial incomprehension, accuses Leventhal of ruining his life and demands recompense. It turns out that Leventhal once obtained a job interview with Allbee's boss on Allbee's recommendation, but Leventhal lost his cool at the interview and ended up arguing with the boss, who retaliated by sacking Allbee. As a result, Allbee's marriage collapsed, and he is now unemployed and homeless. So there's some justice in Allbee's complaint. He *is* a victim. But he is also a drunken, anti-Semitic bully whose insulting aggression is part pose, part sheer brutality. So Leventhal is Allbee's victim too. This murky relationship in which the two men double for the other as accuser and accused, persecutor and victim, is not simply private. It is a case of how the poles of human existence as Bellow sees them—let's call them creaturely materialism and mystical idealism—variously cross and mix in individuals so as to muddy ethical differences at the level of personality and then to bind different people together. (The opposition between the doomed poet Humboldt, the middlebrow intellectual Charlie Citrine, and the wanna-be gangster Rinaldo Cantabile in *Humboldt's Gift* is perhaps the most developed instance of this kind of codependent doubling—in this case, tripling—in Bellow's oeuvre.) It also becomes clear that Allbee and Leventhal's relation is an exemplary case of the connection between people on which the democratic community is formed.

That's also because Allbee has fallen into the profound alienation that democratic capitalism nurtures. It's not just that, in a chilling phrase that points forward to Bellow's own response to the youth movements of the 1960s, he believes that "it is really as if the children of Caliban were running everything" (129) but that he has lost trust both that social justice exists and that individuals have power over their own lives: "it's all blind movement, vast movement and the individual is shuttled back and forth" (62). Worse still, winners in the ceaseless eddying of success and failure take pleasure in their fellow's misfortune—that pleasure constituting much of what satisfaction in, and attachment to, society now is. In the end, and for all its irrational exorbitance, Allbee's demand of Leventhal is a demand for a rational moral accountability in a system that offers none. And Leventhal reluctantly, minimally acknowledges this, partly because he sees in its very unreasonableness a will to test limits, a will to greatness (72). In those terms, Allbee, a scion of an upper-class WASP family, represents nobility gone wrong.

But in the end, Leventhal's goodness and his bond with Allbee do not rely on his humanity or on his virtue. A Rilkean passage points to this. Leventhal is traveling on the Staten Island Ferry one hot summer day:

> The towers on the shore rose up in huge blocks, scorched, smoky, gray, and bare white where the sun was direct upon them. The notion brushed Leventhal's mind that the light over them and over the water was akin to the yellow revealed in the slit of the eye of a wild animal, say a lion, something inhuman that didn't care about anything human and yet was implanted in every human being too, one speck of it, and formed a part of him that responded to the heat and glare, exhausting as these were, or even to freezing, salty things, harsh things, all things difficult to stand. The Jersey shore, yellow, tawny, and flat, appeared on the right. (44)

Pretty clearly, this moment degrades Novalis's romantic and Spinozan will to find "the semblance of the infinite in the finite." It's a mimetic but not a theatrical experience: Leventhal is reenacting his environment, if barely consciously. His mind is "brushed" by ideas; it does not quite contain them. Here, the polluted Jersey shore acquires leonine qualities (pointing forward in that to Bellow's discomforting novel *Henderson the Rain King*), but only partly out there in the world. Leventhal is recurring to what Bellow elsewhere calls "every man's inner inner-city" (Bellow 1998, 207). He is becoming city and becoming animal in the same moment as the speck of inhumanness that enables his interior repetition of exteriority glimmers in him. It's that speck that enables him to endure "difficult things to stand" and hence to recognize the claims buried in Allbee's obsessive pursuit of him. This acknowledgment is made quite outside the sentimental tradition: Leventhal feels neither empathy nor compassion for Allbee. He loathes him (244). Nonetheless, he does find a proper indifference in himself to Allbee's craziness, an indifference that inhibits his rejection and judgment of his persecutor. For all that, Leventhal's less-than-human relation to Allbee does not save Allbee, who in the novel's last scene is to be found at America's rotten heart—he's become a radio advertising executive drunkenly squiring a onetime Hollywood star to a movie premiere. "She's real nobility," says Allbee, between cynicism and "a terrible look of pain" (Bellow 2008, 263), abusing Bellow's most resonant word. This moment does elicit an avowal of obligation from Allbee: "I owe you something," he says to Leventhal. The insufficient acknowledgment that passes between them at that moment—and that, as I say, is based as much on what is inhuman as on what is human in them—is the glue of the social, the basic stuff of democratic intersubjectivity in a world where democracy becomes all the more necessary as it, more or less, makes life worse, makes it easier for winners in the social churn to love society as a means of vaunting it over those who lose.

The Adventures of Augie March *(1953)*

Bellow's next novel, *The Adventures of Augie March*, was regarded as a turning point for Bellow as a writer. A novel that ostensibly aims to insert itself into literary history as a "great American novel," it tells the story of a poor and illegitimate young man's picaresque passage through the class layers of American society. Augie is Forster's Leonard Bast set free by a "universal eligibility to be noble" (Bellow 1995, 36). He refuses to sell out and get rich like his brother Simon or to take up a Nietzschean lordship over others like his lover Thea Fenchel. He wants to live in the universal true—in service of "truth, love, peace, bounty, usefulness, harmony" (522). But he's also a "Columbus of those near-at-hand" (616), of the local everyday, who ends up merely refusing "to lead a disappointed life" (615).

Robert Penn Warren, the eminent New Critic (and another friend of Bellow's), declared that here Bellow had abandoned a "Flaubertian-Jamesian" modernism for a more open, fluid, American form (Warren 1953).[11] Yet for Bellow himself, and for many others, the novel doesn't work as well as it might (Atlas 2000, 193). That's in part for technical reasons. The novel is damaged by two formal discrepancies. The first is that between Augie as character and Augie as narrator. And the second, which is a version of the first, is between Augie as rhetorician and Augie as allegorical of a generalized democratic selfhood. Bellow reverts to *Dangling Man*'s first-person narration here, but he gives Augie a voice that is quite unlike Joseph's. It's not the studied prose of a reflective and trained intellectual but the expressive, vital prose of democratic talk and intellectuality, a widely distributed, promiscuously communicative native intelligence on which democracy, by some accounts, relies. That intelligence is often expressed in ruminations that edge out toward a sanctioned wisdom. And it deploys a style that expands on the modernist canon of literary rhetoric: it is vivid, concrete, dense, figurative. Yet both the plot and syntax of *Augie March* have also been loosened into a form of that paratactic mode which, since Whitman, has come to signify democracy itself. Such a fusion of modernist objectification and Whitmanesque prolixity allows Augie to register the flow of events, some historical, most not, through which a bright, charming, and optimistic young man committed to his democratic self-sufficiency comes to find the discipline of the ordinary as his "project" (Bellow 1995, 526).

But Augie's rhetoric is also designed to record and to vitalize vernacular life, whether that of the squalid Chicago slums or of consumer capitalism's sumptuary extravagances. In its sheer abundance, its all but endless lists of nouns, adjectives, adverbs, its virtuoso use of tropes, this extraordinary literary language becomes a vehicle for a "mysterious adoration of what occurs" (577). At this point, where the novel in its own romantic way praises the world by intensifying it, something rather unexpected happens. Its very inventiveness comes to serve the nobility that the novel's merely human protagonist desires but never achieves. That is to say, the novel's rhetoric itself becomes the novel's protagonist. All the more so because there's no realistic way in which Augie could express himself in the novel's style: as a character, he's given nothing to make us suppose that he's a particularly skilled writer, and this is not the way anyone practically thinks. There's an irrealism in the language that expresses Augie's own drive to nobility from inside the ordinary and that, for all the misery and meanness Augie observes and experiences, endows the world with a quasi-transcendental, if secular, sparkle and wonder.

That bravura discursive irrealism has a political function too. On the one hand, it's attempting to reconcile the distance between the literary and the democratic subject. Augie, unpersuasively, joins them. By the same stroke, it comes to displace the actual differences and hierarchies of American capitalism and hence, by a sleight of hand, loosens political alienation's grip. (That is clearest in Augie's brief stint as a union organizer, which is treated without any acknowledgment of laborism's role in achieving social justice.) That's not the end of it: it's not just that Augie as character or as allegory of democratic subjectivity can't easily be reconciled to Augie as writerly voice but that Augie as writerly voice swallows up his status as character by making him a register of literary intensification of the world that cannot (as it were) *be* sufficiently in the world actually to experience it. It's not just that, like Disraeli's protagonists, Augie lacks sensibility, that he does not sympathize or feel empathy, or that he seems at some remove from his own feelings.[12] It's that his endless throwing himself into the world, which is also a throwing himself into language, does not typify him sufficiently, fix him sufficiently to form a social self capable of stamping his feelings, thoughts, and sensations as coherent experiences. So what *Augie March* reveals is that the novel of democratic experience requires a residue of a classic-realist—a Scott/Austen/Disraelian characterology dependent upon typification, the social structures for which, it would appear, postwar American democracy is barely supplying. The novel's array of formal devices, in a word, enacts, knowingly or not, cultural democracy's threat to an older social order.

Mr. Sammler's Planet *(1970)*

Mr. Sammler's Planet tells the story of an East European Jewish refugee living in Manhattan, old and penniless, supported by his rich nephew,

Ilya Gruner. Sammler is also an enlightened intellectual who, before the war, lived in London, where he befriended and admired progressives like H. G. Wells. But his wartime experiences were horrific: he was left for dead by the Germans in a mass grave next to his wife's corpse and then almost murdered by Polish partisans, surviving against all odds only after being sheltered along with his daughter by a generous Pole. Those events have shattered Sammler's capacity to engage the world, including his faith in Wellsian efforts to explain it. He is not in the technical sense *alienated*; rather, he is detached. He survives in neutrality. The novel, which takes place over a few weeks of the spring in the present-day (around 1967), traces a stage in his reengagement of the world, first as he finds himself intervening on what he perceives to be the license and barbarism of the 1960s youth liberation movement, which are exemplified for him in his niece and nephew as well as to a lesser degree in his now forty-year-old eccentric daughter, and then as he finds himself fascinated by a bold, expensively dressed African American pickpocket working the public transportation system, an emblem of danger and risk in a modernity turned against itself.

I wish first briefly to focus on a quasi-religious moment that occurs to Sammler, as is usual with Bellow, in a precisely defined location: West Fifteenth Street in Manhattan, as he is walking from Stuyvesant Square to the Union Square subway. Sammler is thinking about his daughter, who has stolen a manuscript about moon exploration from a visiting South Asian scientist, Govinda Lal, in the deluded belief that this will help her father write a memoir about his friendship with Wells. And he's also thinking about his nephew Elya, who is dying of an aneurism.

> Meantime too there was in Sammler's consciousness a red flush. Possibly due to Elya Gruner's condition. This assumed a curious form, that of a vast crimson envelope, a sky-filling silk fabric, the flap fastened by a black button. He asked himself whether this might not be what mystics meant by seeing a mandala, and believed the suggestion might have been implanted by association with Govinda, an Asiatic. (Bellow 2004, 94)

This is not a mystical experience proper: it's a vague hallucination that Sammler immediately and banally enough attempts to account for, despite his often-professed animus toward explanation. But very quickly it becomes, if not a full-blown mystical experience, then an intense, simultaneously intellectual, sensory, and spiritual (or, as we might say, existential) experience that signifies the will to, and impossibility of, sustained mysticism within the established tradition for Sammler.

> Through Fifteenth Street ran a warm spring current. Lilacs and sewage. There were as yet no lilacs, but an element of the savage gas was velvety and sweet, reminiscent of blooming lilac. All about was a softness of perhaps dissolved soot, or of air passed through many human breasts, or metabolized in multitudinous brains, or released from as many intestines, and it got to one—oh, deeply, too! . . . For a certain period Mr. Sammler had resisted such physical impressions—being wooed almost comically by momentary and fortuitous sweetness. For quite a long time he had felt that he was not necessarily human. Had no great use, during that time, for most creatures. Very little interest in himself. . . . But then, ten or twelve years after the war, he became aware that this too was changing. In the human setting, along with everyone else, among particulars of ordinary life he was human—and, in short, creatureliness crept in again. Its low tricks, its doggish hind-sniffing charm. So that now, really, Sammler didn't know how to take himself. He wanted, with God, to be free from the bondage of the ordinary and the finite. A soul released from Nature, from impressions, and from everyday life. For this to happen God Himself must be waiting, surely. And a man who has been killed and buried should have no other interest. He should be completely disinterested. Eckhart said in so many words that God loved disinterested purity and unity. . . . What besides the spirit should a man care for who has come back from the grave? However, and mysteriously enough, it happened, as Sammler observed, that one was always, and so powerfully, so persuasively, drawn back to human conditions. So that these flecks within one's substance would always stipple with their reflections all that a man turns toward, all that flows about him. The shadow of his nerves would always cast stripes, like trees on grass, like water over sand, the light-made network. It was a second encounter of the disinterested spirit with fated biological necessities, a return match with the persistent creature. (95–96)

This is a passage that bears more attention than we can give it here. The mandala's "red flush" disappears into the dirty Manhattan spring, a seductive chaotic sensory plenum, poisonously sweet, democratic in the precise sense that no passerby can quite avoid it (it's indifferent to rank) and in which once again the inorganic and the organic mutate into each other. Immersion into this urban detritus triggers Sammler's recognition that his efforts at detachment, his efforts to free himself "from the bondage of the ordinary and the finite" and, in the ascetic quietist manner, to ally himself with God's distant sovereignty over the world (which, for him, characterizes mystics like Meister Eckhart) have come undone and that the "persistent creature" is recapturing him. But his is not a humanist creatureliness, not the humanity of a Kantian committed to moral autonomy and dignity for example, but an animal humanness of "low tricks . . . doggish hind-sniffing charms," the thought of which deliquesces into another cleansing neurological mysticism embedded in the transitory and mundane, where "the shadow of his nerves" will "cast stripes like trees on grass, like water over sand" in a "light-made network" and that accepts that no transcendent order guides us and that we are cast into interiority's reflexive mimicry of exteriority.

This passage too, then, does not quite present illuminations of any divinity; even in its biological turn, it represents memories, thoughts, imaginations, flights in terms, let us quickly add, that, for all their immanentism, resonate with the high Western intellectual tradition, at a point where secular intensities are partly phrased through a traditional religious apprehension. Thus, for instance, Sammler's juxtaposition of lilacs and sewage, his will to sovereignty and sense of an "encounter of the disinterested spirit with fated biological necessities" bear signs of having been influenced not just by a mystical tradition (Eckhart, Saint John of the Cross, Saint François de Sales, Madame de Guyon, Fénelon) but also by the (connected) writings of "George Bataille and other theorists" who embrace the spiritual power of the grotesque, rotten, and perverse and whom, we will later learn, Sammler has been reading on his niece's recommendation, presumably unhappily.

At any rate, this passage poses a critical challenge: Given that it reports the abstract thoughts of a well-read intellectual, and one who no longer trusts ideas, his own or anyone else's, where does its literary vividness come from? First, technically, by the occulted intimacy between the third-person narration and Sammler himself, an intimacy deriving from the fungibility of their narrative functions, which comes to extend to us as readers too. There's a real sense in which the fiction invites and allows us to stand where Sammler now is, to join a community bound by a willingness and capacity to experience intensely, if vicariously, and think hard and concretely from within the character's and narrator's shared intellectual and mystical lineage. That is, the fictionality that separates, say, Eliot's and Disraeli's representations from everyday life and experience is being dissolved, just because no idealized social imaginary can be affirmed. And, second, just from the quality of

Sammler's thought, the way in which his sensations, perceptions, and emotions flow so easily and freshly into the abstract language of philosophical speculation in phrases such as "So that these flecks within one's substance would always stipple with their reflections all that a man turns toward." For all its philosophical and "spiritual" underpinnings, that's a recognizable literary language (turning around the rare use of "stipple" as a transitive verb), sanctioned by modern literary criticism, if here turned to a subtly subversive end, as it explores what Bataille called "the will to proceed to the end of the possible," the limits of being *in* the world, humanly (Bataille 1988, 12). This is true even if Sammler's mimetic mysticism, unlike Bataille's, retains a certain faith in the passage of inner experience to peace and unity. The passage's ambitiousness will likely be welcomed most by those familiar with, or trained in, the literary tradition—let's say from Wordsworth to Blanchot. And to speak sociologically for a moment (for reasons that will become apparent), in 1970 that readership still belonged to a fraction of the wider professional-managerial class, whose historical moment of triumph was exactly the 1960s, when its identity was, at least partly, still bound to humanist pedagogy.[13] Sociologically, if not wholly in spirit, Sammler's mystical moment (a moment, better, when mysticism and humanism undo each other) as *literature* is less than democratic.

Herzog *(1964)*

Many critics believe that *Herzog* is Bellow's most fully achieved fiction. It is not just the critics who think so: the novel was a best seller. Its market success tells us something important about Bellow's place in the postwar literary field, I think. In broad terms, *Herzog* continues the project of Bellow's earlier fictions. It's another exploration of the relation between ordinariness and nobility in an America that is, however, judged still more harshly than in previous texts. And the novel once again resists modernism's "adversary intention" (to use Lionel Trilling's famous phrase). It questions high culture's claims for itself. This refusal of what it sees as the cultural politics of modernism does not make it a middlebrow book, however, if we think of middlebrow writing as repackaging and softening high-cultural topoi for a wider, less committed readership. After all, *Herzog* was at the cutting edge in the terms and means with which it explored the connection, crucial for literary writing, between everyday life and intellectual culture as the humanities presented it. In effect, it occupies a position that cannot be assigned by the logic that ranks culture into high, middle, and low. And it doesn't belong to late twentieth-century "literary fiction" either, as a member of that commodified genre alongside other commodified genres. Rather, as it strains once more to reconcile the literary to cultural democracy, it belongs to a literary space where the commercial/popular and the experimental/recondite can make equal claims to seriousness. We can think of that space as the product of the worn-out remnant of enlightened democratic pedagogy, of the promise of a universal postcompulsory liberal-arts education, the promise that democratized culture will remain in touch with the canonical literary heritage. But, in effect and as we will see, it tells the story of a loss of trust in that promise, a story of democratic experience severing from the sensibilities nurtured in the humanities. At any rate, more obviously than its predecessors and like Forster's texts, *Herzog* is a fictional act of instruction very much directed to its moment. But in resisting, first, the general communicability of philosophic ideas and programs and, second, the notion that ideas can influence conduct, it turns against the conditions of its own popularity and hence releases itself into a new, if provisional, fold in the literary field.

Formally, the novel returns to the intimate third-person narration of *The Victim*, an intimacy all the greater because *Herzog* is often autobiographical. And it revises the rhetoric of *Augie March*. It's still a style loosely based on the canon of New Criticism, determined to vivify experiences as part of its desire to affirm ordinariness and nobility together. But it is no longer based on paratactic vitalist exuberance. Rather, at the level of the sentence it has taken something from the great populist French writer (and extreme racist) Louis-Ferdinand Céline, whose slangy emphatic periods are typically joined together not in Whitmanesque pantheistic celebration but as if in response to the contingent flow of everyday life as mediated through ferocious feelings, usually of complaint and anger. Céline wrote his fictions in the first person; here the third person relays Moses Herzog's no less skittish, spontaneous, emotional engagement through a film of reflective distance. But it is the timing of Herzog's shifts of attention and mood that matter most. The breaks in his cascade of memories, philosophical meditations, fits of self-consciousness, and imaginary acts of communication to others create continual shocks, surprises, anticipations, and disorientations that compel the reader's entry into the novel. The rhythm of those sequences, as much as the rhetoric itself, registers the intensity of the ordinary, but it does so without allowing the writing itself to displace the protagonist, as happened in *Augie March*. That's all the easier because Herzog is a trained, if obsessive, intellectual, and thus his personal life can't easily be emptied of ideas and messages.

As an example of how the style works, take this passage where Herzog travels by train through New Jersey, which is reminiscent of the scene from *The Victim* quoted above. He has been reading a Blanchotian passage of Kierkegaard's *Sickness unto Death* about the impossible experience of death.

> He closed the book as the train reached the junk heaps of New Jersey. His head was hot. He found coolness by pressing the large Stevenson button on his lapel to his cheek. The smoke in the car was sweet, rotten, rich. He sucked it deep into his lungs—a stirring foulness; he raptly breathed in the swampiness of old pipes. The wheels were speeding with a sharp racket, biting the rails. The cold fall sun flamed over the New Jersey mills. Volcanic shapes of slag, rushes, dumps, refineries, ghostly torches, and presently the fields and woods. The short oaks bristled like metal. The fields turned blue. Each radio spire was like a needle's eye with a drop of blood in it. The dull bricks of Elizabeth fell behind. At dusk Trenton approached like the heart of a coal fire. Herzog read the municipal sign—TRENTON MAKES, THE WORLD TAKES!
>
> At nightfall, in cold electric glitter, came Philadelphia.
>
> Poor fellow, his health was not good. (Bellow 2007a, 521–522)

The sentences are now short, emphatic: they don't so much enchant and sparkle the world as dehumanize and industrialize it. Now sweetness and rottenness inhabit the inorganic world, too. But the norms of a modernized prose organized around the canons of academic criticism remain in place: Herzog's interior state is described through a known and knowable external world, which is both object and experience. The details heap up: the coolness of the Adlai Stevenson campaign button minimalizes a moment into a sensation, the train wheels that are defamiliarized when they metaphorically "bite" the tracks cast vividness into the prose in an insistently literary fashion, and the Trenton that approaches "like the heart of a coal fire" joins Herzog's fevered condition to an intimation of hellishness. Jersey's industrial landscape is mirrored in the inorganic trees and fields, and if Herzog does not quite become the built environment here—he's too removed from the world for that—its metallic rottenness gets into him: it stirs and intoxicates him. And his surprising, slightly inept turn to self-judgment, "Poor fellow, his health was not good," enacts that remoteness because of its mildness in comparison to the "cold electric glitter," "volcanic shapes of slag," and so on.

Herzog is undergoing a nervous breakdown. His wife, Madeleine, has divorced him after encouraging him to quit his university post and to spend his inheritance on buying a run-down house in the remote Berkshires, where he was supposed to write his magnum opus, a history of cultural democratization against "the merely aesthetic critique of modern history" (491). Much worse, Herzog has discovered that, during their marriage, Madeleine was having an affair with his best friend Valentine Gersbach. In the present-day of the narration, he is back living in his decayed Berkshire country house, narcissistically prey to memories and recriminations. He recalls how, after Madeleine left him, he traveled to Europe on a lecture tour during which he had some unsatisfactory affairs and how he then moved to New York, where he taught an adult education class and lived in a rented kitchenette on Seventeenth Street while starting a relationship with Ramona, a sexually adept flower-shop proprietor. He remembers how, after a profoundly disturbing scene in a courtroom where he was confronted by the abject misery of the poor, he flew to Chicago intending to murder Madeleine and Valentine. But on seeing Valentine treating his child with loving gentleness, Herzog gave up on that crazy notion and decided to return to his Berkshire house, where he now is. His brother has just visited him to encourage him to hospitalize himself. Refusing, he's awaiting a visit from Ramona at the novel's end.

Throughout his breakdown Herzog is constantly writing letters that he does not send and rarely even writes down. Seeing himself intermittently and megalomaniacally as a charismatic Weberian prophet, a synthesizer of a "new gestalt" (Bell 1979, 161), he writes to famous people, dead and alive (Heidegger, Martin Luther King, Nehru, Adlai Stevenson, Nietzsche . . .). Without obvious rhyme or reason, he also writes to his family lawyer, to his academic colleagues, to acquaintances, family, and friends. These letters are obviously symptomatic: irrational repetitions of the letter he received informing him of his wife's betrayal with Valentine. But they are also distorted pedagogical communications, in the place of those that could happen were transparent, rational, dialogic exchange possible in American public life.

The difficulty goes deeper than that, however, since, according to Herzog himself, in contemporary America, "personal life" has "nothing to fill it with" (Bellow 2007a, 542). That lack deepens and interiorizes the absence of concrete images of the good life under democratization that Disraeli had long ago already discerned. And here it seems caused by two linked processes. First, by the extreme theatricalization and spectacularization of the life-world, of which Valentine is both an example and a victim. He's a poseur, a phony who models himself on Herzog and whose considerable powers as an actor have been perverted into means of self-aggrandizement. Even a destitute male prostitute, arrested for stealing from a client, takes his court appearance as an occasion for a dramatic performance. The second main cause of the emptying of personal experience is nothing other than, to use Shils's term, the "intellectualization" of American life itself (Shils 1972, 82). The democratization of higher education has led to the dominance of Paul Valéry's "delirious professions," professions based on images and ideas and hence to easy, clichéd ideas blocking access to the true and the real by making false accusations against modern society and its "dehumanization" (490–491). Herzog's delirious juggling with ideas in a stream of letters, like the academic monograph he is failing to write, are designed to provide the terms on which a private life might be filled, using as an instrument those very forces—complex ideas that should be taught across the democratic citizenry—that are emptying that life. The literary sensibility is becoming disjunct from democratic life, paradoxically because it too is being democratized.

What seems to stand in place of a stable and full interiority against inchoate public life and massified critical thought is the family, which, however, contains reserves of petty tyranny, as it did in *Augie March*. But family life too is now subject to democratization. The hidden cause of Herzog's nervous breakdown—it is also an ethical collapse—is Madeleine's claim to equality with him, which, looking back, anticipates the organized feminism that transformed society in the 1970s. Madeleine wants a career and does not want to play the covered wifely role. And, albeit less threateningly, Ramona asserts her right to sexual pleasure, too. Madeleine's claims in particular are insupportable to Herzog, and the novel is complicit with his outrage insofar as its narrative technique bars access to Madeleine's thoughts and feelings, even if the reader can't help speculating about what those thoughts and feelings might be, in a way that also ironizes Herzog. At any rate, it's these assaults on Herzog's sense of order that seem to stimulate a social conservatism missing from Bellow's earlier work. Nowhere is this clearer than when we are told that the academic book that Herzog is writing contains an oxymoronic chapter on the "American gentleman," which aims to justify the will of "emergent plebeian classes" "to inherit the aristocratic dignity of the old regimes, which in the modern age might have claimed the right to speak of decline" (492). Herzog's appeal to gentlemanliness, reminiscent of Disraeli's, for instance (and which seems partly cribbed from Leo Strauss's strange 1962 essay "Liberal Education and Responsibility," where the roles of the philosopher and the gentleman merge), is new to Bellow. And the word "dignity" helps contextualize it: it is as if Bellow's play between ordinariness and nobility, between alienation and affirmation, is grounded on not democracy as such but on a certain civic republicanism—a scorn for merely personal relationships (Bellow 2007a, 511); a strong impulsion toward civil order; and an ethics of manly courage, restraint, loyalty, that is, Ciceronian *dignitas*. But that ethic operates more as criterion of judgment than as a practical guide for living or as an ideal that might stabilize collective life. It too belongs to the dizziness, the muddle of intellectual life, as democracy is radically extended.

In the end, the novel, even more than Bellow's earlier fictions, offers no closure. There's no rational happy self that even a saner Herzog might inhabit, exactly because his delirium fits the democratic condition so well. Strangely enough, then, the novel's last paragraphs contain a (probably unintentional) reminiscence of the end of *Howards End*. In the Berkshire house, Herzog is awaiting Ramona for dinner, who's bringing a bottle of wine:

> Coming back from the woods, he picked some flowers for the table. He wondered whether there was a corkscrew in the drawer. Had Madeleine taken it to Chicago? Well, maybe Ramona had a corkscrew in her Mercedes. An unreasonable thought. A nail could be used, if it came to that. Or you could break the neck of the bottle as they did in old movies. Meanwhile, he filled his hat from the rambler vine, the one that clutched the rainpipe. The spines were still too green to hurt much. By the cistern there were yellow day lilies. He took some of these, too, but they wilted instantly. And, back in the darker garden, he looked for peonies; perhaps some had survived. But then it struck him that he might be making a mistake, and he stopped, listening to Mrs. Tuttle's sweeping, the rhythm of bristles. Picking flowers? He was being

> thoughtful, being loveable. How would it be interpreted? (He smiled slightly.) Still, he need only know his own mind, and the flowers couldn't be used; no, they couldn't be turned against him. So he did not throw them away. He turned his dark face toward the house again. He went around and entered from the front, wondering what further evidence of his sanity, besides refusing to go to the hospital, he could show. Perhaps he'd stop writing letters. Yes, that was what was coming, in fact. The knowledge that he was done with these letters. Whatever had come over him during these last months, the spell, really seemed to be passing, really going. He set down his hat, with the roses and day lilies, on the half-painted piano, and went into his study, carrying the wine bottles in one hand like a pair of Indian clubs. Walking over notes and papers, he lay down on his Recamier couch. As he stretched out, he took a long breath, and then he lay, looking at the mesh of the screen, pulled loose by vines, and listening to the steady scratching of Mrs. Tuttle's broom. He wanted to tell her to sprinkle the floor. She was raising too much dust. In a few minutes he would call down to her, "Damp it down, Mrs. Tuttle. There's water in the sink." But not just yet. At this time he had no messages for anyone. Nothing. Not a single word. (348)

This is a more rational Herzog than we have seen hitherto. Admittedly, he's still slightly manic, picking the vine and putting it in his hat for a floral arrangement (and he's waiting for a woman who runs a flower shop!). And for all his self-consciousness, he's disassociated, persuading himself against the evidence that he's being thoughtful, lovable in his flower gathering. Then, too, his decision to stop writing letters seems more a performance of sanity than a sign of it. But still: he's more deliberative and sensitive to other people's responses to him than he has been.

What does this ending mean? Most obviously, there's no grand moment of reconciliation here. No moment like that in which Allbee recognized his debt to Leventhal, or in which Joseph submitted to the discipline of the ordinary, or in which Augie finds the power in himself not to live a disappointed life. Rather, like the ending of *Howards End*, this is an ambiguous, almost casual turn toward the pastoral. We know that animals have invaded the Berkshire house, that Herzog does not want to banish them, that the screen is being collapsed by the vine, that the dust is thick and rising. The human world is lapsing into a nonhuman one, this time the world not of industry but of wild and sovereign nature. But this nature is not, like Forster's wych elm or hay, proleptic of a possible democratic community to come. Herzog's Berkshire house will shelter no dehierarchized loving community against society. On the contrary: the novel ends with Herzog settling back into private life, embracing a quotidian kind of lordship by handling the wine bottles "like a pair of Indian clubs" and preparing to give a servant an order—a master's authority over a servant being probably the relationship most resistant to liberal and democratic ordering, even in the United States (see Orren 1991 on the legal basis of this relationship and its implications).

I have been arguing that Bellow too is a radical democrat, writing in and of the structures prophesized by Tocqueville and driven to displace community as a practical goal by a redemptive, if delirious, nobility of spirit harnessed to those sensibilities, understandings, and forms of association that are under threat in democratic intellectual life. But that seems barely in evidence in this last paragraph. Yet Herzog does not succumb to the discipline of the ordinary, either. The challenge posed by this strangely muted ending is best met by emphasizing Herzog's silence: it is as if, in a turn of considerable formal neatness and ingenuity, the silence that follows the story's end is where the significance of the novel is largely to be located. Herzog is retreating from communicability to a reduced lordship. He's giving up on pedagogy, on improvement, on reform, we might want to say. He seems to be farewelling that overextended, overvalued selfhood against which Daniel Bell warned. But having said this, the novel's ending does not impose a retrospective and final meaning upon it. Rather, it marks a pause in the flow of that discourse—neither public nor private—whose capacity simultaneously to make life better than it is and to cover life with general and repetitious ideas is a key problem for democracy as equality. More than that, it is a silence that accedes to a society that is at an endpoint, because there is nowhere except more democracy to go. And it can also acknowledge that liberty and equality ceaselessly peter out in the mundane world where knowledge fails, compulsions move, strength is tested, orders are to be given, and where the desire for, and recognition of, the will to nobility and greatness cannot be contained.

So Bellow is another conservative democrat, Tocqueville's heir, but is deeply suspicious of alienation and critique and the smugness and idealism that they can encourage. He is also a degraded pantheist, precariously balancing at humanism's limits, driven toward mysticism. And as a novelist, he has no interest in any reformist agenda or indeed in any formal politics even if, at least from *Herzog* on, he is unable fully to sustain either a refusal of refusal or a retreat into neutrality. This is an extremely uncomfortable but, as I hope this chapter has shown, also a compellingly disabused position. My argument has been that Bellow's struggle with the deep insufficiencies of democracy leads him toward providing fictional images of everyday life from the perspective—more or less—of a well-read, high-minded humanities professor struggling to affirm the democratic world despite the betrayal and disorder he everywhere encounters not least through his own professional tools and purposes. Everyday life—intimacy itself—turns out to be anything but sustaining for trust and hope, but, treated like this, it also comes to provide the content and form through which the power of literature to present the chastening truth about democratic capitalism can be triumphantly proved. It might even provide occasions for a greatness untarred by narcissism. Yet it needs, impossibly, to be proved as an experience rather than as an idea or as a form or even as a will, just because when democracy becomes fundamental, our connection to the long literary heritage is frayed.

NOTES

1. DEMOCRACY TODAY

1. One reason for this increased attention is that the Soviet Union's collapse in 1989 loosened restrictions on expressing dissatisfaction with our democratic system.

2. The next couple of pages, like the opening pages of the next chapter, are interspersed with revised passages that first appeared in chapter 7 of During (2010), but now in the service of a different argument.

3. I owe the phrase "market state" to Bobbitt (2008, 88ff.).

4. My choice of name should be obvious from what follows. In terms of its history, George Gissing long ago used the term "democratic capitalism" against socialism (see Gissing 2009, 563); for the Marxist concept of the "capitalist state," see Jessop (2002); for the slightly different concept of "state capitalism," see Pannekoek (1936).

5. My sense of Pentecostalism's social drives relies on Martin (2008).

6. For the loss of faith in political democracy from the 1970s on, see Rodgers (2011, 88). But for a convincing account, which makes the case that historically in the United States parties were very rarely based on principles, see Laski (1949, 72ff.). This too is less true elsewhere in the West.

7. In the West, China is thought of as antidemocratic, but its current political system is more properly to be considered as just another mode of democratic state capitalism. It is also ideologically attached to popular sovereignty and equality, but its "democracy" component happens not to be organized as a liberal system in which different groups or interests are represented in the legislature via political parties. Nor does it make a hard, nondemocratic distinction between the legal and political branches of government.

8. Dissidence to democracy on the left, albeit an ambiguous dissidence, seems largely confined to antistatist autonomist groups, who inherit versions of political anarchism and associationalism and who combine a commitment to

equality with a rejection of state governmentality (see, e.g., Raunig 2010). Wholehearted right-wing antidemocratic thinking is today rarely expressed in public.

9. For theodicy's "bourgeois" character, see Geuss (2009, 174–179).

10. Other ways of conceiving of cultural democracy are possible, of course. In particular, there is the argument that the cultural uses of the modern media and the Internet extend social participation in ways that themselves constitute a mode of democratization, or at least of what John Hartley calls "democratainment" (that is, the fusion of entertainment and democratic participation). See Hartley (2007, 132ff.). And for a persuasive critique of his position, see Turner (2010, 44–46). My thanks to Catherine Driscoll for drawing my attention to this literature.

11. See Jay (2005) for an excellent history of this. And see Westbrook (1991, x–xi), for John Dewey's particularly influential version of it.

12. For the evidence that inequality hinders growth, see Wilkinson and Pickett (2009).

13. An illuminating defense of a left conservatism is to be found in Gerald Cohen's "A Truth in Conservatism: Rescuing Conservatism from the Conservatives," which I recommend reading in its original lecture form, easily findable on the Web. Although echoes of his wonderful turns of phrase may be heard in this introduction, I am not persuaded of his implied thesis that it is in itself conservative (even with a small c) to resist instrumental reason and to endorse "particular things." Rather, conservatism endorses particular patterns, traditions, institutions, habits, and so on. The "particular thing," however, often worth defending against improvement or utility, is a shibboleth, rather, of a certain liberalism.

2. REFORM OR REFUSAL? LIVING IN DEMOCRATIC CAPITALISM

1. My understanding of the 1688 revolution owes something to Pincus (2009) and his view that James II's Catholic absolutism, modeled on Louis XIV and Gallicanism, represented a competing mode of modernization to the Whig one. For the background of the "duty to resist" in the Reformation, see Skinner (1978, 2:189–349).

2. It's true that in the early 1980s Foucault did begin to show an interest in Athenian democracy as a result into his investigations into different conditions under which the power to speak the truth becomes possible. See Foucault (2010).

3. The most detailed and subtle account of the background of these lectures that I know is to be found in Tribe (2009), where a rich account of the (mainly secondary and very topical) literature that Foucault called upon is to be found. Tribe, however, stops short of my conclusion that Foucault appreciates neoliberalism. I thank Ryan Walter for this reference.

4. Polanyi's thesis that the modern concept of "society" was first deployed in early nineteenth-century England has to be distinguished from, and is not in contradiction to, claims that a more abstract "rise of the social" occurred toward the end of the seventeenth century (on the back of philological interest in the history of various legal systems, according to Pocock 2011).

5. Tribe thinks Foucault's failure to make this point is just oversight: he "does not really spell out . . . that the [neoliberal] form of governmentality simply eradicates the public domain" (Tribe 2009, 694).

6. Let's take Stendhal as an example. His novels were routinely dismissed for about fifty years after his death because of their "inhumanity," as Amiel's widely read diaries put it (Amiel 1905, 2:292). It's no accident that critics associated with Action Française played an important role in Stendhal's rehabilitation.

7. My information on Action Française is mainly based on Weber's still standard account in Weber (1962).

8. There is an extensive literature on Eliot's relation to French ultra-rightism. See, for instance, Asher (1995), Chace (1973), and North (1991).

9. The accounts of this formation that I prefer are to be found in Kessler (2001) and Loubet del Bayle (1969). Much of the historiography of this movement (and notably Nolte 1996 and Sternhell 1995) is interested in arguing that it is actually a kind of fascism. I am skeptical about this, in part because "fascism" carries such a heavy negative moral weight that it crushes important distinctions requiring careful analysis.

10. With the exception of Michael Holland, most critics have preferred to understand Blanchot either as a literary metaphysician or as a negative theologian. But however useful such accounts can be, they miss his work's crucial dynamic. For two insightful accounts of Blanchot in this spirit, see Hart (2004) and Hill (1997).

11. For Maulnier, see Carroll (1995, 222–247), Antliff (2007, 203–246), and Sanos (2006). My reading of Maulnier differs significantly from Carroll's. I say that this understanding is new, and in a certain sense it is, but it belongs to the intellectual (and political) history, in which Sorel is a key figure, and which has been expertly evacuated in Antliff.

12. In the early 1940s, Blanchot wrote a "chronicle of intellectual life" for the pro-Vichy *Journal des Débats*, a journal whose readership had long been mainly confined to the ultra-right and by which he had been employed since the beginning of his career. See Bident (1998, 181).

3. CONSERVATISM AND CRITIQUE

1. See Geuss (2009, i–xiii), Attali (2007), Wolin (2008), and Brown (2010).

2. That relations between democracy and capitalism are contingent is indicated, for instance, in Ellen Meiksins Wood's (1991, 105) argument that, from

the late nineteenth century on, Germany was more successful as a capitalist state than the United Kingdom because "precapitalist" state formations prevented the economy from being as thoroughly exposed to mass consumer markets. Similar logics may be at work in China today.

3. A fuller account of what critique has meant and means today would need to absorb recent developments in the "sociology of critique" as carried out most prominently by Luc Boltanski, which attempts to provide pathways between vernacular and empirical complaint and discontent and rational/theoretical critique on the back of a compelling understanding of the history and sociology of critique. See Boltanski (2011).

4. Horkheimer (1947) elaborates on this connection.

5. Illuminating scholarship on conservatism includes Compagnon (2005), Hirschman (1991), Levigne (1994), Nash (1976), and O'Sullivan (1976).

6. For an extension of Schmitt's claims for Malebranche's influence into de Bonald's conservative social thought, see Milbank (2006, 58ff.).

7. For Hume's relation to Malebranche, see Phillipson (1989, 38–40). For Hutcheson on Malebranche, see Hutcheson (1994, 63).

8. Hoggart's neglected later works do, however, return to a fairly unabashed conservatism, if a conservativism that is now fighting to preserve social democracy itself. See Hoggart (1996).

4. LITERARY CRITICISM'S FAILURE

1. The book consists largely of essays previously published in the *Quarterly Review*.

2. These pieces were published in book form as *The Sacred Wood* in 1920.

3. Wollheim (1973) cogently analyzes Eliot's dissertation.

4. Later, and especially in his 1926 Clark Lectures, when he was moving toward Christian orthodoxy, he parsed the periodization of the breakup of experience differently. The Florentine trecento (and especially Dante) came to signify Western civilization's most organic moment, not early seventeenth-century England.

5. See Russo (1989) and Fry (2000) for good accounts of Richards as a literary theorist.

6. See Russo (1989).

7. Mulhern (1979) remains the essential account of Leavisism.

8. *Scrutiny* was established in 1933 and lasted for twenty years exactly.

9. See MacKillop (1997, 333–340), for a description of Leavis's response to postwar restructurings of the English education system.

10. For Leavis's denunciation of New Criticism, see Mulhern (1979, 252–253). The first-generation New Critics famously shared a Leavisite nostalgia for the organic society but, most markedly perhaps with Ransom, in the mid-1930s

they moved from an agrarian anti-industrial capitalism to a reconciliation with capitalism. See Janovich (1993). As to Empson: his defense of Richards's analytic methods against John Sparrow is interesting, because there he declares that it is a "necessary assumption" of literary criticism that a "poem conveys very nearly the same experience to extremely different people" while at the same time emphasizing poetry's complex (and transexperiential) intelligence against its capacity to communicate simple feelings. Empson (1930, 475). Also see Russo (1989, 529–531).

11. I borrow "left-conservatism" from Ellis (2008, 107).

12. My sense of Strauss as an exilic and modernist intellectual owes a great deal to the fascinating account in Sheppard (2006).

5. THE LITERARY ORIGINS OF MODERN DEMOCRACY

1. Luciano Canfora argues that this incompatibility is expressed as early as the fifth century BCE in Pericles' famous oration on democracy as reported by Thucydides. Canfora (2006, 7–8).

2. As Claude Lefort (2000) and Pierre Rosanvallon (2001) have shown, no career marks the stakes of the move from liberty to equality at this period more clearly than the French politician and historian François Guizot. But this is already fairly clear in Schmitt's *The Crisis of Parliamentary Democracy*, in which Guizot plays a key role.

3. For Félicité Lamennais, see Vidler (1954). Any fuller list of critical accounts of parliamentary democracy would include, from the right, Belloc and Chesterton (1911) and Schmitt (1985); from social democracy, Michels (1915) and Schumpeter (1942); and from the Marxist left, Adler (1922).

4. Laski exaggerates when he writes, "Tocqueville was really writing a book on French civilization, the US crept into its pages as a source of illustration rather than a central theme" (Laski 1949, 16–17). But one sees what he means. In recent times, Tocqueville's work has mainly (but by no means only) been taken up by conservatives who hope to simultaneously affirm and criticize democratization as he did. On this phenomenon, from the French point of view, see Audier (2008, 169–192).

5. This is clear, for instance, in his correspondence with his friend, the antidemocratic English essayist W. R. Greg; see Morley (1904, 229–231).

6. For the religion of humanity, see Wernick (2001).

7. As Mannheim was to write in 1933, "Dictatorship is not the antithesis of democracy, it represents one of the possible ways in which a democratic society may try to solve its problems" (Mannheim 1956, 172).

8. Of course, conservative communitarianism can still be called on by figures like Norman Podhoretz, Gertrude Himmelfarb, and most recently by Phillip Blond's "Red Tory" movement in Britain.

9. In fact, Disraeli's historiography is rather dependent on that of the Whiggish historian Henry Hallam, as argued in his *Constitutional History of England from the Accession of Henry VII to the Death of George II* (1827), which made the case for the democratic structure of the English monarchy. But it also drew somewhat on his father's work, especially his history of Charles I's reign. See Burrow (1981, 18, 30–31).

10. In its 1840s versions, Disraeli's historiography also leans on William Cobbett's Tory radical *History of the Protestant Reformation*. For Bolingbroke and the Reformation origins of the Whigs and Tories, see Dickinson (1970, 195).

11. It is relevant to note how important private ownership is to Tocqueville's theory of democracy and how important the banning of entail is to its establishment in America.

12. Thus it is no accident that the conservative "new political history" of the 1970s, which insisted on the relative autonomy and influence of high politics, first established itself in Maurice Cowling's analysis of how and why Disraeli passed the Second Reform Act. See Cowling (1967).

13. An implicit foreign politics that Disraeli shared with the Whig Lord Palmerston lies behind his Semitism at this time. He is bolstering sympathy for the Ottoman Empire against Russian expansion.

14. Eliot's most overt entry into the political scene was her preface to *Felix Holt* (1866), where writing in her own voice directly to the working class, she urges them not to pursue power via democracy until they are ready to wield it responsibly.

15. Servants are important in fictions interested in conversational democracy (and in class relations) right up until the present day. See Robbins (1993) for the pathbreaking analysis of the servant's role in nineteenth-century fiction.

6. *HOWARDS END*'S SOCIALISM

1. See Leavis (1978, 276–277), for an influential description of Forster as belonging to "liberal culture."

2. The literature on this is large. Dangerfield (1961) remains useful, but also see Clarke (1978), Searle (1992), Barrow (2006), and Wellhofer (1996).

3. One reason for this sense of confusion was that older forms of national memory were losing credibility by 1910. One thinks, in particular, on the one side, of the liberty-focused Whig histories popularized in the nineteenth century by Macaulay (and which had been so important to Gladstonian liberalism) and, on the other, of Tory-imperialist histories focused on global British glory, popularized by J. A. Froude and J. R. Seeley.

4. This list is drawn from Carpenter (1916, 240). For the historiography of the new age movements, see Pierson (1973), Yeo (1977), and Rowbotham (2010).

5. Rowbotham (2009) has become Carpenter's standard biography. For Carpenter and Forster in relation to sexuality, see Bredbeck (1997) and Martin (1983).

6. Even figures like Eduard Bernstein and the Webbs could make mystical-democracy statements at times. Kloppenberg (1986, 228–229) cites passages that argue that collectivism ties societies to the "beyond."

7. It is worth noting that the concept of the modern that applies to Butler was not what had already appeared in Paris and London in the 1840s and that insisted that the present merited especial attention because it was now unmoored from the past in unprecedented ways. Such a concept appears in Baudelaire's art writing and in Thomas Carlyle's social commentary. Baudelaire (1962, 455); for Carlyle, see LaValley (1968).

8. Furbank (1948) persuasively argues that Butler was a key figure in defining the modern before World War I but that after, and especially after the publication of Malcolm Muggeridge's *Samuel Butler: The Earnest Atheist* (1937), Butler's reputation declined, and he began to be regarded simply as an "eccentric."

9. Temple (2005) offers an excellent account of Edward Wakefield's various emigration projects.

10. The history of genteel manual labor is yet to be written. I don't mean to imply here that it begins in the second half of the nineteenth century: for instance, a character like the benevolent magnate and baronet Thornhill in Oliver Goldsmith's *Vicar of Wakefield* expresses his basic human sympathies by working to harvest hay along with the vicar himself and the family (Goldsmith 2006, 38). But his is voluntary or, rather, leisure labor.

11. Forster's admiration for both Butler and Carpenter are well known. He wrote essays on both. He contemplated writing a book on Butler in the 1910s and gave elements of his character to the elder Mr. Emerson in *A Room with a View*. It was during a visit to Carpenter that he conceived the idea of writing *Maurice*, his openly homosexual novel. His friend Goldsworthy Lowes Dickinson, who had come through the Shelley cult of the 1880s and had tried to live the new-life socialist ideal of the simple life on a cooperative agricultural smallholding, was also an ardent admirer of Carpenter, although Forster's biography of Dickinson is strategically reticent about this matter. For the essay on Carpenter see Forster (1962a, 216–219); for his essay on Butler, see Forster (1962a, 222–226). For his mention of Dickinson's relation to Carpenter, see Forster (1973, 47). There is a small secondary literature on these relations; see, in particular, Copley (2006), Martin (1983), and Holt (1946).

12. "Moral realism" is Lionel Trilling's term: see Trilling (1967, 12). I don't mean to imply that Forster might not also be conceived of as a modernist: Jed Esty (2004, 5), for instance, calls Forster, Woolf, and Eliot the "most canonical

representatives" of English modernism. But, clearly, careful distinctions between Forster and writers like Woolf (or Lawrence or Joyce) may be made.

13. We first meet her at a concert in which Beethoven's Fifth Symphony is being played. She confesses to using the music to create a narrative in her mind, to make the music programmatic, a tendency the novel seems to distance itself from. This scene relies on Nietzsche's *The Birth of Tragedy*, where it represents a triumph of the Apollonian over the Dionysian. See Nietzsche (1999, 35). This is important because Helen is more "Apollonian" than Margaret: that's her problem, but that's what allows her to triumph in the end.

14. It is worth noting that the novel was first published by Edwin Arnold, mainly a textbook publisher.

15. The Wagnerian leitmotif was most notably applied to the English novel by George Meredith in his *One of Our Conquerors*.

7. SAUL BELLOW AND THE ANTINOMIES OF DEMOCRATIC EXPERIENCE

1. For the widespread interest in Tocqueville's work during this period, see Strout (1986).

2. This line of thought was neither new nor, in fact, inherently connected to conservatism: leaving Gramsci's defense of a classical education aside, as early as 1957, from the bohemian left, Bellow's best friend of his youth, Isaac Rosenfeld, had criticized the University of Chicago (excepting the Downtown Basic Program of Liberal Education for Adults) for capitulating to the culture of folk song and cool jazz on terms not unlike Bloom's (Rosenfeld 1962, 336).

3. In service of his conservatism, Bellow became capable of petty acts such as blackballing Edward Said, Amiri Baraka, and Susan Sontag from receiving MacArthur Fellowships (Atlas 2000, 493).

4. See Amis (1995), Hitchens (2006), Eggers (2005), and Wood (2004).

5. The Straussian wing of the conservative movement further argued (like Bell) that the United States' postwar inability to resist policies that extended cultural democracy and mere prosperity was a sign and cause of the nation's cultural deterioration (Levigne 1994, 51ff.).

6. I don't mean to suggest that vividness becomes a key criterion for good literary writing only in twentieth-century New Criticism. It is already there, for instance, in Hugh Blair's *Lectures on Rhetoric and Belles Lettres* (1783).

7. For the insufficiency of the modern soul, see Bellow (1998, 266).

8. For an excellent summary of the *Partisan Review* project, see Collini (2005, 228–230), which also stresses their interest in alienation. See also Wilford (1995).

9. For Bellow's dislike of Leavisism, see Cronin and Siegel (1994, 47).

10. Lionel Trilling noted that "The editors of *Partisan Review* have long been thought to give a rather special credence and sympathy" to alienation (Trilling 1956, 64).

11. And the judgment has stuck, even if, as Tony Tanner has argued, claims of this kind overlook the way in which *Augie March* too is a stunted bildungsroman, a story about its protagonist's path toward affirming the discipline of the common and ordinary (Tanner 1965, 45).

12. The refusal of sympathy is expressed clearly by the Nietzschean Thea Fenchel, who argues that empathy is a "sickness" connected to self-theatricalization (Bellow 1995, 369–370).

13. See Hoberek (2005, 5ff.) for an analysis of the U.S. novel of the time in these terms.

BIBLIOGRAPHY

Adler, Max. 1922. *Die Staatsauffassung des Marxismus. Ein Beitrag zur Unterscheidung von Soziologischer und Juristischer Methode.* Vienna: Wiener Volksbuchhandlung.

Adorno, Theodor. 1998. [1962] "Why Still Philosophy?" In *Critical Models: Interventions and Catchwords.* Trans. Henry W. Pickford. New York: Columbia University Press.

———. 2008. [2003, lectures given 1960–1966] *Lectures on Negative Dialectics.* Ed. Rolf Tiedemann. Trans. Rodney Livingstone. Cambridge: Polity Press.

Adorno, Theodor, and Max Horkheimer. 2010. "Towards a New Manifesto." *New Left Review* 65: 33–63.

Agamben, Giorgio. 2005. *The Time That Remains: A Commentary on the Letter to the Romans.* Stanford, Calif.: Stanford University Press.

Amiel, Henri-Fredric. 1905. *Diaries.* 2 vols. Trans. Mrs. Humphrey Ward. New York: Macmillan and Co.

Amis, Martin. 1995. "A Chicago of a Novel." *Atlantic Monthly*: 114–127.

Antliff, Mark. 2007. *Avant-Garde Fascism: The Mobilization of Myth, Art, and Culture in France, 1909–1939.* Durham, N.C.: Duke University Press.

Arnold, Matthew. 1965. [1869] *Culture and Anarchy with Friendship's Garland and Some Literary Essays.* Ed. R. H. Super. Ann Arbor: University of Michigan Press.

Asher, Kenneth. 1995. *T. S. Eliot and Ideology.* Cambridge: Cambridge University Press.

Atlas, James. 2000. *Bellow: A Biography.* London: Faber and Faber.

Attali, Jacques. 2007. *Une brève histoire de l'avenir.* Paris: Fayard.

Audier, Serge. 2008. *La pensée anti-68: Essai sur les origins d'une restauration intellectuelle.* Paris: La Découverte.

Badiou, Alain. 2006. *Metapolitics.* Trans. Jason Barker. London: Verso.

Balibar, Étienne. 2010. *La proposition de l'égaliberté.* Paris: PUF.

Barrow, Logie. 2006. *Democratic Ideas and the British Labour Movement, 1880–1914.* 2nd ed. Cambridge: Cambridge University Press.

Bataille, Georges. 1988. [1954, 1st ed. 1943] *Inner Experience.* Trans. Leslie Anne Boldt. Albany, N.Y.: SUNY Press.

Battestin, Martin C., with Ruthe R. Battestin. 1989. *Henry Fielding: A Life.* London: Routledge.

Baudelaire, Charles. 1962. *Curiosités esthétiques. L'art romantique et autres oeuvres critiques.* Ed. Henri Lemaître. Paris: Garnier.

Bauer, Bruno. 1882. *Disraelis Romantischer und Bismarcks Sozialistischer Imperialismus.* Chemnitz: Ernst Schmeitzner.

Beauman, Nicola. 1993. *Morgan: A Biography of E. M. Forster.* London: Hodder and Stoughton.

Beck, Ulrich. 1992. [1986] *Risk Society: Towards a New Modernity.* London: Sage.

Bell, Daniel. 1946. "A Parable of Alienation." *Jewish Frontier* 13, no. 11: 12–19.

———. 1971. "The Cultural Contradictions of Capitalism." In *Capitalism Today.* Ed. Daniel Bell and Irving Kristol. New York: New American Library.

———. 1979. *The Cultural Contradictions of Capitalism.* London: Heinemann.

———. 2001. [rev. ed. 1962, 1st ed. 1960] *The End of Ideology.* Cambridge, Mass.: Harvard University Press.

Belloc, Hilaire, and Cecil Chesterton. 1911. *The Party System.* London: Stephen Swift.

Bellow, Saul. 1987. Foreword to *The Closing of the American Mind.* New York: Simon & Schuster.

———. 1995. [1953] *The Adventures of Augie March.* London: Everyman's Library.

———. 1998. [1982] *The Dean's December.* London: Penguin.

———. 2004. [1969] *Mr. Sammler's Planet.* Intro. Stanley Crouch. New York: Penguin.

———. 2007a. *Novels 1956–1964: Seize the Day, Henderson the Rain King, Herzog.* New York: Library of America.

———. 2007b. [1944] *Dangling Man.* New York: Penguin.

———. 2008. [1947] *The Victim.* New York: Penguin.

Benjamin, Walter. 1999. [1933] "Experience and Poverty." In *Walter Benjamin: Selected Writings.* Vol. 2: *1927–1934.* Ed. M. W. Jennings. Cambridge, Mass.: Harvard University Press.

Bident, Christophe. 1998. *Maurice Blanchot: Partenaire invisible. Essai biographique.* Paris: Champ Vallon.

Blackmur, R. P. 1956. *The Lion and the Honeycomb: Essays in Solicitude and Critique.* London: Methuen.

———. 1964. *Eleven Essays in the European Novel.* New York: Harcourt Brace and World.

———. 1983. *Studies in Henry James.* New York: New Directions.

Blanchot, Maurice. 1937. "De la révolution à la littérature." *L'Insurgé* 1: 3.

———. 1986. *The Writing of Disaster.* Trans. Ann Smock. Lincoln: University of Nebraska Press.

———. 1993. [1969] *The Infinite Conversation.* Trans. Susan Hanson. Minneapolis: University of Minnesota Press.

———. 1995. [1949] *The Work of Fire.* Trans. Charlotte Mandell. Stanford, Calif.: Stanford University Press.

———. 2001. [1943] *Faux Pas.* Trans. Charlotte Mandell. Stanford, Calif.: Stanford University Press.

Bloch, Ernst. 2009. *Atheism in Christianity: Religion of Exodus and the Kingdom.* London: Verso.

Bobbitt, Philip. 2008. *Terror and Consent: The Wars for the Twenty-first Century.* London: Allen Lane.

Boltanski, Luc. 2011. *On Critique: A Sociology of Emancipation.* Trans. Gregory Elliott. Cambridge: Polity Press.

Boltanski, Luc, and Eve Chiapello. 2006. *The New Spirit of Capitalism.* Trans. Gregory Elliott. London: Verso.

Bousquet, Marc. 2008. *How the University Works: Higher Education and the Low-Wage Nation.* New York: New York University Press.

Bradley, F. H. 1962. [1927, 1st ed. 1876] *Ethical Studies.* Oxford: Oxford University Press.

Brans, Jo. 1979. "Common Needs, Common Preoccupations: An Interview with Saul Bellow." In *Critical Essays on Saul Bellow*, ed. Stanley Trachtenberg. Boston: G. K. Hall and Co.

Braverman, Harry. 1974. *Labor and Monopoly Capitalism: The Degradation of Work in the Twentieth Century.* New York: Monthly Review Press.

Bredbeck, Gregory W. 1997. "'Queer Superstitions': Forster, Carpenter, and the Illusion of Sexual Identity." In *Queer Forster*, ed. Robert K. Martin and George Piggford. Chicago: University of Chicago Press.

Brooks, Cleanth. 1947. *The Well Wrought Urn.* New York: Harcourt Brace and World.

Brown, Wendy. July 20, 2010. "We Are All Democrats Now . . . ." *Theory & Event* 13.2 Project MUSE. University of Queensland Library, Brisbane, QLD, Australia.

Burke, Edmund. 1990. [1792] "Letter to Sir Hercules Langrishe." In *Miscellaneous Writings*, ed. E. J. Payne. Library of Economics and Liberty 2. December 2010. http://www.econlib.org/library/LFBooks/Burke/brkSWv4c6.html.

Burrow, J. W. 1981. *A Liberal Descent: Victorian Historians and the English Past.* Cambridge: Cambridge University Press.

Butler, Samuel. 1914. *A First Year in Canterbury Settlement, with Other Early Essays.* London: A. C. Fifield.

Byron, George Gordon. 1974. *Letters and Journals.* Ed. Leslie A. Marchand. 12 vols. Cambridge, Mass.: Harvard University Press.

Canfora, Luciano. 2006. *Democracy in Europe: A History.* Trans. Simon Jones. Oxford: Blackwell Publishing.

Carpenter, Edward. 1916. *My Days and Dreams; Being Autobiographical Notes.* London: George Allen and Unwin.

Carroll, David. 1995. *French Literary Fascism: Nationalism, Anti-Semitism, and the Ideology of Culture.* Princeton, N.J.: Princeton University Press.

Chace, William. 1973. *The Political Identities of Ezra Pound and T. S. Eliot.* Stanford, Calif.: Stanford University Press.

Chomsky, Noam. 1977. "Bellow's Israel." *New York Arts Journal*: 29–32.

Clarke, Peter. 1978. *Liberals and Social Democrats.* Cambridge: Cambridge University Press.

Cole, G. D. H. 1948. *Samuel Butler.* London: Morrison & Gibb.

Collini, Stefan. 1993. *Public Moralists: Political Thought and Intellectual Life in Britain, 1850–1930.* New ed. Oxford: Oxford University Press.

———. 2005. *Absent Minds: Intellectuals in Britain.* Oxford: Oxford University Press.

Collins, J. Churton. 1891. *The Study of English Literature: A Plea for Its Recognition and Organization at the Universities.* London: Macmillan.

Compagnon, Antoine. 2005. *Les antimodernes de Joseph de Maistre à Roland Barthes.* Paris: Éditions Gallimard.

Constant, Benjamin. 1988. [1819] "The Liberty of the Ancients Compared with That of the Moderns." In *Political Writings*, ed. Biancamaria Fontana. Cambridge: Cambridge University Press.

Copley, Antony. 2006. *A Spiritual Bloomsbury: Hinduism and Homosexuality in the Lives and Works of Edward Carpenter, E. M. Forster, and Christopher Isherwood.* Lanham, Md.: Lexington Books.

Cowling, Maurice. 1967. *1867: Disraeli, Gladstone and Revolution: The Passing of the Second Reform Bill.* Cambridge: Cambridge University Press.

Critchley, Simon. 2007. *Infinitely Demanding: Ethics of Commitment, Politics of Resistance.* London: Verso.

Cronin, Gloria L., and Ben Siegel. 1994. *Conversations with Bellow.* Jackson: University of Mississippi Press.

Dangerfield, George. 1961. [1935] *The Strange Death of Liberal England.* New York: Capricorn.

Dawson, Christopher. 1939. *Beyond Politics.* London: Sheed & Ward.

de Man, Paul. 1979. *Allegories of Reading: Figural Language in Rousseau, Nietzsche, Rilke, and Proust.* New Haven, Conn.: Yale University Press.

Derrida, Jacques. 1992. *Acts of Literature.* Ed. Derek Attridge. New York: Routledge.

———. 2006. *The Politics of Friendship.* Trans. George Collins. London: Verso.

Dewey, John. 2008. [1925] *The Later Works of John Dewey, 1925–1953.* Vol. 1: *Experience and Nature.* Carbondale: Southern Illinois University Press.

Dickinson, H. T. 1970. *Bolingbroke.* London: Constable.

Disraeli, Benjamin. 1853. Preface to *Vivian Grey*, Rev. edition. London: Longmans, Green and Co.

———. 1913. [1835] *Whigs and Whiggism.* Ed. and intro. William Hutcheon. London: John Murray.

———. 1927. *The Bradenham Edition of the Novels and Tales of Benjamin Disraeli, 1st Earl of Beaconsfield.* Intro. Philip Guedella. 12 vols. London: Peter Davies.

Dunn, John. 2005. *Democracy: A History.* New York: Atlantic Monthly Press.

During, Simon. 2010. *Exit Capitalism: Literary Culture, Theory, and Post-Secular Modernity.* London: Routledge.

Eggers, Dave. 2005. "Saul Bellow: Novelists and Critics Remember an American Master." *Slate.* http://www.slate.com/id/2116446/.

Eliot, George. 1900. [1858] *Scenes of Clerical Life.* New York: Mershon Company.

Eliot, T. S. 1927. "Literature, Science, and Dogma." *The Dial* 82: 239–243.

———. 1928. *The Sacred Wood.* London: Methuen.

———. 1960. *Christianity and Culture.* New York: Harvest Books.

———. 1964. [1915] *Knowledge and Experience in the Philosophy of F. H. Bradley.* London: Faber and Faber.

———. 1965. *To Criticize the Critic.* London: Faber and Faber.

———. 1994. *The Varieties of Metaphysical Poetry.* Ed. Ronald Schuchard. London: Faber and Faber.

Ellis, Charlie. 2008. "Relativism and Reaction: Richard Hoggart and Conservatism." In *Richard Hoggart and Cultural Studies*, ed. Sue Owen. London: Palgrave.

Empson, William. 1930. "O Miselle Passer!" *Oxford Outlook* 10: 470–478.

Esty, Jed. 2004. *A Shrinking Island: Modernism and National Culture in England.* Princeton, N.J.: Princeton University Press.

Forster, E. M. 1962a. [1951] *Two Cheers for Democracy.* New York: Mariner Press.

———. 1962b. [1927] *Aspects of the Novel.* Harmondsworth: Penguin.

———. 1973. [1934] *Goldsworthy Lowes Dickinson and Other Writings.* London: Edward Arnold.

———. 1998. [1910] *Howards End.* Ed. Paul B. Armstrong. New York: Norton.

Foucault, Michel. 1994. *Dits et écrits.* 4 vols. Paris: Éditions Gallimard.

———. 1996. *Foucault Live.* New York: Autonomedia.

———. 2008. *The Birth of Biopolitics: Lectures at the Collège de France, 1978–1979.* Ed. Michel Senellart. Trans. Graham Burchell. London: Palgrave Macmillan.

———. 2010. *The Government of the Self and Others: Lectures at the Collège de France, 1982–1983.* Ed. Michel Senellart. Trans. Graham Burchell. London: Palgrave Macmillan.

Fraser, Russell. 1979. "R. P. Blackmur: The Politics of a New Critic." *Sewanee Review* 87, no. 4: 557–572.

Fry, Paul H. 2000. "I. A. Richards." In *The Cambridge History of Literary Criticism*. Vol. 7: *Modernism and the New Criticism*. Cambridge: Cambridge University Press.

Furbank, P. N. 1948. *Samuel Butler*. Cambridge: Cambridge University Press.

Gauchet, Marcel. 1989. *La révolution des droits des hommes*. Paris: NRF.

———. 2007. *L'avènement de la démocratie*. Vol. 1: *La révolution moderne*. Paris: Éditions Gallimard.

Geroulanos, Stefanos. 2010. *An Atheism That Is Not Humanist Emerges in French Thought*. Stanford, Calif.: Stanford University Press.

Geuss, Raymond. 2005. *Outside Ethics*. Princeton, N.J.: Princeton University Press.

———. 2009. *Politics and the Imagination*. Princeton, N.J.: Princeton University Press.

Giddens, Anthony. 1994. *The Third Way: The Renewal of Social Democracy*. Cambridge: Polity Press.

Gissing, George. 2009. [1880] *Demos*. Project Gutenberg e-book 4309. Release date December 9.

Goldsmith, Oliver. 2006. *The Vicar of Wakefield*. New York: Oxford University Press.

Hart, Kevin. 2004. *The Dark Gaze: Maurice Blanchot and the Sacred*. Chicago: University of Chicago Press.

Hartley, John. 2007. *Television Truths: Forms of Knowledge in Popular Culture*. Malden, Mass.: Blackwells.

Hayek, Friedrich. 1944. *The Road to Serfdom*. Chicago: University of Chicago Press.

Hess, Moses. 2004. *The Holy History of Mankind and Other Writings*. Ed. Shlomo Avineri. Cambridge: Cambridge University Press.

Hill, Leslie. 1997. *Blanchot: Extreme Contemporary*. London: Routledge.

Hirschman, Albert O. 1991. *The Rhetoric of Reaction*. Cambridge, Mass.: Harvard University Press.

Hirst, Paul. 1994. *Associative Democracy*. Amherst: University of Massachusetts Press.

Hitchens, Christopher. 2006. Foreword to *The Adventures of Augie March*. New York: Penguin.

Hoberek, Andrew. 2005. *The Twilight of the Middle Class: Post–World War II American Fiction and White-Collar Work*. Princeton, N.J.: Princeton University Press.

Hobhouse, L. T. 1911. *Liberalism*. New York: H. Holt.

Hoggart, Richard. 1996. *The Way We Live Now*. London: Chatto & Windus.

Holt, Lee Elbert. 1946. "E. M. Forster and Samuel Butler." *PMLA* 61, no. 3: 804–819.

Horkheimer, Max. 1947. "Means and Ends." In *The Eclipse of Reason*. New York: The Seabury Press.

———. 1972. *Critical Theory: Selected Essays.* Trans. Matthew J. O'Connell. New York: Herder and Herder.

Horn, Gerd-Rainer. 2007. *The Spirit of '68: Rebellion in Western Europe and North America, 1956–1976.* New York: Oxford University Press.

Howe, Irving. 1946. "The Lost Young Intellectual." *Commentary* (October): 361–362.

Hulme, T. E. 2004. *The Collected Writings of T. E. Hulme.* Ed. Karen Csengeri. Oxford: Oxford University Press.

Hutcheson, Francis. 1994. *Philosophical Writings.* London: Dent.

Inglehart, Ronald, and Christian Welzel. 2005. *Modernization, Cultural Change, and Democracy: The Human Development Sequence.* Cambridge: Cambridge University Press.

James, C. L. R. 1993. *American Civilization.* Ed. Anna Grinshaw and Keith Hart. Oxford: Blackwells.

James, Henry. 1991. [1886] *The Princess Casamassima.* London: Everyman.

James, William. 2000. [1904] "A World of Pure Experience." In *Pragmatism and Other Writings*, ed. Giles Gunn. New York: Penguin.

Janovich, Mark. 1993. *The Cultural Politics of the New Criticism.* Cambridge: Cambridge University Press.

Jay, Martin. 2005. *Songs of Experience: Modern European and American Variations on a Universal Theme.* Berkeley: University of California Press.

Jessop, Bob. 2002. *The Future of the Capitalist State.* Cambridge: Polity Press.

Judt, Tony. 2010. *Ill Fares the Land.* New York: Penguin.

Keane, John. 2009. *The Life and Death of Democracy.* New York: W. W. Norton & Company.

Kearney, Anthony. 1986. *John Churton Collins: The Louse on the Locks of Literature.* Edinburgh: Scottish Academic Press Ltd.

Kessler, Nicolas. 2001. *Histoire politique de la Jeune Droite (1929–1942): Une révolution conservatrice à la française.* Paris: L'Harmattan.

Kloppenberg, James T. 1986. *Uncertain Victory: Social Democracy and Progressivism in European and American Thought, 1870–1920.* New York: Oxford University Press.

Kojève, Alexandre. 1956. "Françoise Sagan." *Critique* 111: 702–708.

Kramer, Hilton. 1999. [1994] "Saul Bellow, Our Contemporary." In *The Twilight of the Intellectuals: Culture and Politics in the Era of the Cold War.* Chicago: Ivan R. Dee.

Kristol, Irving. 1971. "'When Virtue Loses All Her Loveliness.'" In *Capitalism Today*, ed. Daniel Bell and Irving Kristol. New York: New American Library.

Laski, Harold. 1921. *Foundations of Sovereignty.* New York: Harcourt, Brace & Co.

———. 1949. *The American Democracy.* London: George Allen and Unwin.

Lasserre, Pierre. 1902. *La morale de Nietzsche*. Paris: Société de Mercure de France.

———. 1908. *Le romantisme français*. Paris: Société de Mercure de France.

Latour, Bruno. 1993. *We Have Never Been Modern*. Trans. Catherine Porter. Cambridge, Mass.: Harvard University Press.

LaValley, Albert J. 1968. *Thomas Carlyle and the Idea of the Modern*. New Haven, Conn.: Yale University Press.

Leavis, F. R. 1943. *Education and the University: A Sketch for an "English School."* London: Chatto and Windus.

———. 1962. [1932] *New Bearings in English Poetry*. Harmondsworth: Penguin.

———. 1978. [1952] *The Common Pursuit*. Harmondsworth: Penguin.

Lecky, William. 1981. [1896] *Democracy and Liberty*. 2 vols. Indianapolis, Ind.: Liberty Fund.

Lefort, Claude. 2000. "Guizot: Polemical Liberal." In *Writing: The Political Text*. Ed. and trans. David Ames Curtis. Durham, N.C.: Duke University Press.

Levigne, Robert. 1994. *Recasting Conservatism: Oakeshott, Strauss, and the Response to Postmodernism*. New Haven, Conn.: Yale University Press.

Loubet del Bayle, Jean-Louis. 1969. *Les non-conformistes des années 30*. Paris: Éditions du Seuil.

Loving, Jerome. 1999. *Walt Whitman: The Song of Himself*. Berkeley: University of California Press.

MacKillop, Ian. 1997. *F. R. Leavis: A Life in Criticism*. New York: St. Martin's Press.

Manent, Pierre. 1996. *Tocqueville and the Nature of Democracy*. Lanham, Md.: Rowman and Littlefield.

Mannheim, Karl. 1940. *Man and Society in an Age of Reconstruction*. London: Kegan Paul, Trench, Trubner.

———. 1943. *Diagnosis of Our Time: Wartime Essays of a Sociologist*. London: Kegan Paul.

———. 1956. *Essays on the Sociology of Culture*. Ed. Ernest Manheim. London: Routledge Kegan Paul.

———. 1997. [1925–1927] *Conservatism: A Contribution to the Sociology of Knowledge*. Trans. David Kettler and Volker Meja. London: Routledge.

Marginson, Simon, and Mark Considine. 2000. *The Enterprise University: Power, Governance and Reinvention in Australia*. Melbourne: Cambridge University Press.

Martin, David. 2008. *Pentecostalism: Their World, Their Parish*. New York: Wiley-Blackwell.

Martin, Robert K. 1983. "Edward Carpenter and the Double Structure of Maurice." *Journal of Homosexuality* 8, no. 3/4: 35–46.

Marx, Karl. 1985. *Early Writings*. Ed. Lucio Colletti. Trans. Rodney Livingstone. London: Penguin.

Maulnier, Thierry. 1925. *Nietzsche*. Paris: Éditions Gallimard.

———. 1943. *Lecture de Phèdre*. Paris: Éditions Gallimard.

———. 1947. [1935] *Racine*. Paris: Éditions Gallimard.

Melville, Herman. 2008. [1851] *Moby Dick*. Ed. Tony Tanner. New York: Oxford University Press.

Michels, Robert. 1915. *Political Parties: A Sociological Study of the Oligarchical Tendencies of Modern Democracy*. New York: Hearst International Library.

Milbank, John. 2006. *Theology and Social Theory*. 2nd ed. Oxford: Blackwell.

———. 2009. "On Baseless Suspicion: Christianity and the Crisis of Socialism." In *The Future of Love: Essays in Political Theology*. Eugene, Ore.: Cascade Books.

Montety, Étienne de. 1994. *Thierry Maulnier. Biographie*. Paris: Julliard.

Morley, John. 1904. "W. R. Greg: A Sketch." In *Critical Miscellanies*. Vol. 3. New York: Macmillan.

Moyn, Samuel. 2010. *The Last Utopia: Human Rights in History*. Cambridge, Mass.: Harvard University Press.

Mulhern, Francis. 1979. *The Moment of "Scrutiny."* London: Verso.

———. 2000. *Culture/Metaculture*. London: Routledge.

Nairn, Tom. 1988. *The Enchanted Glass: Britain and Its Monarchy*. London: Verso.

Nancy, Jean-Luc. 1991. *The Inoperative Community*. Minneapolis: University of Minnesota Press.

———. 2005. *La déclosion (Déconstruction du christianisme, I)*. Paris: Éditions Galilée.

Nash, George. 1976. *Conservative Intellectual Movements in America*. New York: Basic Books.

Needham, John. 1982. *The Completest Mode: I. A. Richards and the Continuity of English Literary Criticism*. Edinburgh: University of Edinburgh Press.

Newfield, Christopher. 2008. *Unmaking the Public University*. Cambridge, Mass.: Harvard University Press.

Nietzsche, Friedrich. 1999 [1871]. *The Birth of Tragedy*. Ed. Raymond Geuss and Ronald Speirs. Trans. Ronald Speirs. Cambridge: Cambridge University Press.

Nolte, Emile. 1966. *Three Faces of Fascism: Action Française, Italian Fascism, National Socialism*. Trans. Leila Vennewitz. New York: Holt, Rinehart and Winston.

North, Michael. 1991. *The Political Aesthetic of Yeats, Eliot, and Pound*. Cambridge: Cambridge University Press.

Oakeshott, Michael. 1933. *Experience and Its Modes*. Cambridge: Cambridge University Press.

Orren, Karen. 1991. *Belated Feudalism: Labor, the Law, and Liberal Development in the United States*. New York: Oxford University Press.

Orwell, George. 1968. *The Collected Essays, Journalism, and Letters of George Orwell*. Vol. 2: *My Country Right or Left, 1940–1943*. London: Secker and Warburg.

O'Sullivan, Noel. 1976. *Conservatism*. London: Dent.

Palmer, D. J. 1965. *The Rise of English Studies: An Account of the Study of English Language and Literature from Its Origins to the Making of the Oxford English School.* Oxford: Oxford University Press.

Pannekoek, Anton. 1936. "State Capitalism and Dictatorship." http://www.marxists.org/archive/pannekoe/1936/dictatorship.htm. Accessed September 2010.

Phillipson, Nicholas. 1989. *Hume*. New York: St. Martin's Press.

Pierson, Stanley. 1973. *Marxism and the Origins of British Socialism: The Struggle for a New Consciousness*. Ithaca, N.Y.: Cornell University Press.

Pincus, Steve. 2009. *1688: The First Modern Revolution*. New Haven, Conn.: Yale University Press.

Pocock. J. G. A. 2011. "Historiography as a Form of Political Thought." *History of European Ideas* 37: 1–6.

Polanyi, Karl. 1957. [1944] *The Great Transformation: The Political and Economic Origins of Our Time*. Boston: Beacon.

Potter, Rachel. 2006. *Modernism and Democracy: Literary Culture 1900–1930*. Oxford: Oxford University Press.

Proudhon, Pierre-Joseph. 1887. *System of Economical Contradictions, or the Philosophy of Misery*. Trans. Benjamin. R. Tucker. Boston: Benjamin Tucker.

Rancière, Jacques. 1999. *Disagreement: Politics and Philosophy*. Minneapolis: University of Minnesota Press.

———. 2006. *Hatred of Democracy*. Trans. Steve Corcoran. London: Verso.

———. 2009a. *The Emancipated Spectator*. Trans. Gregory Elliott. London: Verso.

———. 2009b. *Et tant pis pour les gens fatigués: Entretiens*. Paris: Éditions Amsterdam.

———. 2010. *Dissensus: On Politics and Aesthetics*. Ed. and trans. Steven Corcoran. London: Continuum.

Ransom, John Crowe. 1955. "The Concrete Universal: Observations on the Understanding of Poetry." In *Poems and Essays*. New York: Vintage Books.

Raunig, Gerald. 2010. *A Thousand Machines*. Trans. Aileen Dierig. New York: Semiotext(e).

Richards, I. A. 1926. *Science and Poetry*. New York: W. W. Norton and Co.

———. 1928. [1924] *Principles of Literary Criticism*. Rev. ed. London: Routledge Kegan Paul.

———. 1929. *Practical Criticism*. London: Routledge, Kegan Paul.

Robbins, Bruce. 1993. *The Servant's Hand: English Fiction from Below*. Durham, N.C.: Duke University Press.

Rodgers, Daniel T. 2011. *Age of Fracture*. Cambridge, Mass.: Harvard University Press.

Rorty, Richard. 1998. *Achieving Our Country: Leftist Thought in Twentieth-Century America.* Cambridge, Mass.: Harvard University Press.

Rosanvallon, Pierre. 2001. *Le moment Guizot.* Paris: Éditions Gallimard.

———. 2008a. *La légitimé démocratique.* Paris: Éditions du Seuil.

———. 2008b. *Counter-Democracy: Politics in an Age of Distrust.* Trans. Arthur Goldhammer. Cambridge: Cambridge University Press.

Rosenfeld, Isaac. 1962. [1957] "Life in Chicago." In *An Age of Enormity,* ed. Ted Solotaroff. Cleveland and New York: World Publishing Company.

Rousseau, Jean-Jacques. 1973. *The Social Contract and the Discourses.* Ed. and trans. G. D. H. Cole. London: J. M. Dent and Sons.

Rowbotham, Sheila. 2009. *Edward Carpenter: A Life of Liberty and Love.* London: Verso.

———. 2010. *Dreamers of a New Day: Women Who Invented the Twentieth Century.* London: Verso.

Runciman, W. G. 2005. *Pluralism and the Personality of the State.* Cambridge: Cambridge University Press.

Russo, John Paul. 1989. *I. A. Richards: His Life and Work.* Baltimore, Md.: The Johns Hopkins University Press.

Sanos, Sandrine. 2006. "'From Revolution to Literature': The Political Aesthetics of the Young New Right, 1936–1937." *Contemporary French and Francophone Studies* 10: 1, 85–95.

Schmitt, Carl. 1985. [1923] *The Crisis of Parliamentary Democracy.* Trans. Ellen Kennedy. Cambridge, Mass.: The MIT Press.

———. 1986 [first ed. 1919, rev. ed. 1925]. *Political Romanticism.* Trans. Guy Oakes. Boston: The MIT Press.

———. 1996. [1929] "The Age of Neutralizations and Depoliticizations." In *The Concept of the Political,* trans. Tracy B. Strong. Chicago: University of Chicago Press.

Schumpeter, Joseph A. 1950 [1942]. *Capitalism, Socialism, Democracy.* New York: Harper and Row.

Searle, G. R. 1992. *The Liberal Party: Triumph and Disintegration, 1886–1929.* London: Macmillan.

Seidman, Michael. 2004. *The Imaginary Revolution: Parisian Students and Workers in 1968.* Oxford: Berghahn Books.

Sen, Amartya. 2000. *Development as Freedom.* New York: Anchor Books.

Shapiro, Ian. 2003. *The State of Democratic Theory.* Princeton, N.J.: Princeton University Press.

Sheppard, Eugene, R. 2006. *Leo Strauss and the Politics of Exile: The Making of a Political Philosopher.* Waltham, Mass.: Brandeis University Press.

Shils, Edward. 1972. *The Intellectual and the Powers and Other Essays.* Chicago: University of Chicago Press.

Skinner, Quentin. 1978. *The Foundations of Modern Political Thought.* 2 vols. Cambridge: Cambridge University Press.

———. 1998. *Liberty Before Liberalism.* Cambridge: Cambridge University Press.

Slaughter, Sheila, and Gary Rhoades. 2004. *Academic Capitalism and the New Economy.* Baltimore, Md.: The Johns Hopkins University Press.

Smith, Adam. 1993. [1776] *The Wealth of Nations.* Ed. Kathryn Sutherland. Oxford: Oxford University Press.

Sorel, Georges. 1999[1906]. *Reflections on Violence.* Ed. Jeremy Jennings. Cambridge: Cambridge University Press.

Sternhell, Zeev. 1995. *Neither Right nor Left: Fascist Ideology in France.* Trans. David Maisel. Princeton, N.J.: Princeton University Press.

Strauss, Leo. 1995. [1959] "What Is Liberal Education?" In *Liberalism Ancient and Modern*, ed. Allan Bloom. Chicago: University of Chicago Press.

Strout, Cushing. 1986. "Tocqueville and the Idea of an American Literature (1941–1971)." *New Literary History* 18, no. 1: 115–127.

Surin, Kenneth. 2009. *Freedom Not Yet: Liberation and the Next World Order.* Durham, N.C.: Duke University Press.

Tanner, Tony. 1965. *Saul Bellow.* Edinburgh: Oliver and Boyd.

Temple, Philip. 2005. *A Sort of Conscience: The Wakefields.* Auckland: University of Auckland Press.

Thibaudet, Alfred. 1913. "L'esthétique des trois traditions." *NRF* (1913): 5–42.

Tilly, Charles. 2004. *Contention and Democracy in Europe, 1650–2000.* Cambridge: Cambridge University Press.

Tillyard, E. M. W. 1958. *The Muse Unchained.* London: Bowes and Bowes.

Tocqueville, Alexis de. 1955. [1856] *The Ancien Régime and the French Revolution.* Trans. Stuart Gilbert. London: Fontana.

———. 1966. [1835, 1840] *Democracy in America.* Trans. George Lawrence. New York: Harper & Row.

Tønder, Lars, and Lasse Thomassen, eds. 2005. *Radical Democracy: Politics Between Abundance and Lack.* Manchester: Manchester University Press.

Tribe, Keith. 2009. "The Political Economy of Modernity: Foucault's Collège de France Lectures of 1978 and 1979." *Economy and Society* 38: 679–698.

Trilling, Lionel. 1956. [1952] "The Situation of the American Intellectual at the Present Time." In *A Gathering of Fugitives.* Boston: Beacon Press.

———. 1967. [1943] *E. M. Forster: A Study.* London: Hogarth Press.

Turner, Graeme. 2010. *Ordinary People and the Media: The Demotic Turn.* London: Sage.

Ure, Andrew. 1835. *The Philosophy of Manufactures: or, An Exposition of the Scientific, Moral, and Commercial Economy of the Factory System of Great Britain.* London: Charles Knight.

Verdès-Leroux, Jeannine. 1996. *Refus et violences: Politique et littérature à l'extrême droite des années trent aux retombées de la Libération.* Paris: Éditions Gallimard.

Vidler, A. R. 1954. *Prophecy and Papacy: A Study of Lamennais, the Church, and the Revolution.* New York: Scribners.

Wang, Hui. 2003. *China's New Order: Society, Politics, and Economy in Transition.* Cambridge, Mass.: Harvard University Press.

Warren, Robert Penn. "The Man with No Commitments." *New Republic* 2 (November 1953): 22–23.

Weber, Eugen. 1962. *Action Française: Royalism and Reaction in Twentieth-Century France.* Stanford, Calif.: Stanford University Press.

Weimann, Robert. 1974. *"New Criticism" und die Entwicklung burgerlicher Literaturwissenschaft: Geschichte und Kritik autonomer Interpretationsmethoden.* München: Verlag Ch. H. Beck.

Wellhofer, E. Spencer. 1996. *Democracy, Capitalism and Empire in Late Victorian Britain, 1885–1910.* London: Macmillan.

Wernick, Andrew. 2001. *Auguste Comte and the Religion of Humanity: The Post-Theistic Program of French Social Theory.* Cambridge: Cambridge University Press.

Westbrook, Raymond. 1991. *John Dewey and American Democracy.* Ithaca, N.Y.: Cornell University Press.

Whitman, Walt. 1982. *Complete Poetry and Collected Prose.* New York: Library of America.

Wilford, Hugh. 1995. *The New York Intellectuals: From Vanguard to Institution.* Manchester: Manchester University Press.

Wilkinson, Richardson, and Kate Pickett. 2009. *The Spirit Level: Why More Equal Societies Almost Always Do Better.* London: Allen Lane.

Williams, Bernard. 2007. "The Idea of Equality." In *In the Beginning Was the Deed: Realism and Moralism in Political Argument.* Princeton, N.J.: Princeton University Press.

Williams, Raymond. 1950. *Reading and Criticism.* London: Frederick Mueller.

———. 1958. *Culture and Society: 1780–1950.* London: Chatto & Windus.

———. 1983. "Cambridge English: Past and Present." In *Writing in Society*. London: Verso.

Wolin, Sheldon. 2003. *Tocqueville Between Two Worlds: The Making of a Political and Theoretical Life.* Princeton, N.J.: Princeton University Press.

———. 2008. *Democracy Incorporated: Managed Democracy and the Specter of Inverted Totalitarianism.* Princeton, N.J.: Princeton University Press.

Wollheim, Richard. 1973. "Eliot and F. H. Bradley." In *On Art and the Mind: Essays and Lectures.* London: Allen Lane.

Wood, Ellen Meiksins. 1991. *The Pristine Culture of Capitalism: A Historical Essay on Old Regimes and Modern States.* London: Verso.

Wood, James. 2004. "Saul Bellow's Comic Style." In *The Irresponsible Self: On Laughter and the Novel.* New York: Farrar, Straus and Giroux.

Yeo, Stephen. 1977. "A New Life: The Religion of Socialism in Britain: 1883–1896." *History Workshop* 4: 5–56.

Zipperstein, Steven J. 2009. *Rosenfeld's Lives: Fame, Oblivion, and the Furies of Writing.* New Haven, Conn.: Yale University Press.

INDEX